RATIONAL EGOISM

RATIONAL EGOISM THE MORALITY FOR HUMAN *Flourishing*

Craig Biddle

Glen Allen Press
Richmond, Virginia

Book typography by Pete Masterson, Aeonix Publishing Group

Published by Glen Allen Press, P.O. Box 5274, Glen Allen, VA 23058

ISBN: 978-0-9713737-1-6

Educational organizations are eligible for special discounts on bulk purchases of this book. Please contact the publisher for information.

Printed in the United States of America

Acknowledgments

The essays in this book initially were published in *The Objective Standard* over the course of several years, and a number of different assistant or associate editors provided helpful comments along the way. In particular, I want to thank Alan Germani, Joshua Lipana, Ari Armstrong, Jon Hersey, and Tim White for their comments on one or more of these essays. Thanks also to my crack copy editor, Joanne Foster, for her many corrections and improvements.

Thank you, Sarah Biddle, for reading and improving all of these articles, as you do with practically everything I write. Thank you, Elliott Hill, for preparing the index. And thank you, Pete Masterson, for laying out the book and designing its cover.

Finally, and emphatically, I want to thank Ayn Rand and Leonard Peikoff for teaching me about Objectivism and rational egoism and for helping me to do "the simplest thing in the world."

Contents

Introduction

If you want to flourish—if you want to make your life the best, happiest, most fulfilling life it can be—you need a moral code geared to that purpose.

This book is about the only moral code that is.

To maximize your happiness across the full span of your life, you need a morality that provides principled guidance for your thoughts and actions with respect not only to your short-range needs, but also to your long-range needs; and not only to your material needs, but also—and more fundamentally—to your spiritual needs: the needs of your mind, your rational faculty, and your emotional faculty.

Rational egoism is the only moral code that provides such guidance.

As you will see in the pages ahead, the principles of rational egoism are derived from observations and integrations of the factual requirements of human life and happiness. But because we all have been told from the moment we could listen that "self-interest is bad" and "self-sacrifice is good," most people regard the morality of self-interest as a contradiction in terms.

It is not.

Indeed, the contradiction, as this book also demonstrates, is the idea that being moral consists in self-sacrificially serving others. In addition to learning why self-interest is moral, you'll learn why being moral does not—and logically cannot—mean sacrificially serving others.

That's right. The conventional views of morality have it exactly backward. And the consequences of accepting those views have been and continue to be materially and spiritually devastating to human beings—individually, socially, and politically.

Rational egoism—or rational self-interest—is the name that Ayn Rand gave to the moral code of her philosophy, Objectivism. This book examines, concretizes, and illuminates various aspects of that morality—from its basis in perceptual reality, to its fundamental values and virtues, to its personal and social applications, to its extension into politics as the principle of individual rights, and to its support of a fully free, fully civilized, fully rights-protecting society.

Rational Egoism: The Morality for Human Flourishing consists of a dozen essays originally published in *The Objective Standard* and organized here in a manner that will help you to understand (or fortify your understanding) of this morality by means of your own observations and integrations. After reading it, you will understand (or better understand) the principles of this code, how to apply them and thrive accordingly, and how to communicate them clearly and convincingly to others.

So, if you want to flourish, if you want to know why that's the *right* thing to do, and if you want to convey this radical truth to others, turn the page. This book is for you.

1

The Beauty of Ayn Rand's Ethics

Ayn Rand opposed the morality of self-sacrifice, which is inherent in most philosophic systems and all religions. She advocated instead a morality of self-interest—the Objectivist ethics—which, as she explained in her essay "Causality Versus Duty," is neatly summed up by the Spanish proverb "God said: 'Take what you want, and pay for it.'"[1]

Rand was an atheist, so her use of "God" here is metaphorical. By "God said" she means "reality dictates." She is referring to the immutable fact that if you want to achieve an effect (an end), you must enact its cause (the means). This is the law of causality applied to human values. Our values—whether a wonderful career, a romantic relationship, good friendships, life-enhancing hobbies, or political freedom—do not come to us automatically, nor do we pursue them automatically. If we want these things, we must choose to act in certain ways and not in others. This is the way reality is. This principle is an *absolute*. "God said."

"Take what you want" refers to the fact that human values are *chosen*. The realm of human values—the realm of morality—is the realm of choice. A proper morality is not about "divine commandments" (there is no God) or "categorical imperatives" (there's no such thing) or "duties" (they don't exist). Rather, it is about what you want out of life and what you must do to get what you want. A proper morality is a set of principles to guide your choices and actions toward a lifetime of happiness.

Importantly, as Rand emphasized, this does not make morality subjective. What promotes a person's life is dictated not by his feelings divorced from facts, but by the factual requirements of his life and happiness—given his nature as a human being. Just as a rabbit can't live and prosper by jumping off cliffs, and just as an eagle can't live and prosper by burrowing underground, so a person can't live and prosper by acting contrary to the requirements of *his* life.

We are complex beings of body and mind, matter and spirit, and the requirements of our life and happiness derive from both aspects of this integrated whole. If we want to know what these requirements are, we must identify the relevant facts. Given our nature, we need certain values in order to live and prosper. We need material values such as food, clothing, shelter, and medicine; we need spiritual values, such as self-respect, self-confidence, friendship, and romantic love; and we need political values, such as the rule of law and political freedom—which enable us to pursue our material and spiritual values. Consequently, in order to live and prosper, we must uphold and employ the one *fundamental* value that makes our identification and pursuit of all our other values possible: reason.

Reason is our means of observing reality, forming concepts, identifying causal relationships, avoiding contradictions, and forming principles about what is good and bad for our life. Reason is our only means of knowledge and our basic means of living. Thus, if our goal is a lifetime of happiness, we must uphold reason as an absolute; we must be rational as a matter of principle.

Being rational doesn't mean never erring; humans are fallible beings, and occasional errors are part of life. Nor does it mean repressing or ignoring one's feelings; that would not be rational, as feelings are a crucial kind of fact. Rather, being rational means committing oneself, as a matter of principle, to identifying the available and relevant facts concerning one's alternatives in life, to acting on one's best judgment given what one knows at any given time, and to correcting any errors one commits if and when one discovers them.

Seen in this light, "Take what you want" doesn't mean: "Go by your emotions without respect for facts and logic." It means: "Use your rational judgment to figure out which goals and courses of action will result in a lifetime of happiness, and proceed accordingly." It means: "Take what you *rationally* want."

"Pay for it" refers to the fact that if we want to achieve our goals, we must *work* to achieve them, we must *enact* their causes. So says the law of causality. This is not a burden but a blessing: Choosing values and working to achieve them—whether a career in computer programming, a romantic relationship with the girl or guy of our dreams, a sailing trip around the world, or a summer home in the Catskills—is not a process to bemoan. It is part and parcel of living a wonderful life.

A proper morality is a crucial tool for living and loving life, and the Objectivist ethics is just such a morality. Its values of reason, purpose, and self-esteem—along with its virtues of rationality, productiveness, honesty, integrity, independence, justice, and pride—are, one and all, in service of this end. They are our means of taking what we want and paying for it.

Such is the beauty of the Objectivist ethics.[2]

2

Secular, Objective Morality: Look and See

Thinking is man's only basic virtue, from which all the others proceed. And his basic vice, the source of all his evils, is . . . the refusal to think—not blindness, but the refusal to see; not ignorance, but the refusal to know. —Ayn Rand

You've heard it countless times and in various forms: "If there is no God, there is no objective morality"—"If there is no God, anything goes"—"If there is no God, 'good' and 'evil' have no objective meaning"—and so on.

But that notion is demonstrably false and morally disastrous.

Objective morality does not depend on the existence of "God." And that's a good thing, too. Among other reasons: (a) There is no evidence for the existence of God, which is why no one has ever provided such evidence. And (b) according to the scriptures of each of the three major religions—Judaism, Christianity, and Islam—God commands murder, commits mass murder, condones slavery, authorizes rape, and sanctions other atrocities.[1]

Further, morality based on commandments is not objective but *subjective*; it is based on assertions issued by the alleged ruling consciousness; thus, whatever that consciousness commands—whether to love your neighbor or to beat your wife or to murder unbelievers—is "moral" simply because he said so. That is the very essence of subjectivity.

Objective morality comes not from revelation, faith, or divine commandments—but from observation, logic, and the laws of nature.

Morality (or ethics) is a code of values intended to guide people's choices and actions.[2] This is true of *all* moralities, whether religious or secular. As to which morality is objectively correct, that depends on which one corresponds to the facts that give rise to the need of morality.

Either we need morality, or we don't. If we don't need it, then we don't need it, and there is no point in pursuing the subject at all.[3] If, on the other hand, we *do* need morality, then identifying the reason *why* we need it will help us to understand which values are objectively correct and which are not.

Because morality is a code of *values*, in order to understand why people need it we must first understand what values are and why people need them. This is why the philosopher Ayn Rand began her inquiry into morality with the questions: What are *values*? And why do people need them?[4] We'll follow Rand's approach and take these questions in turn.

What are values? Looking at reality, we can see that values are the things one acts to gain or keep.[5] For instance, you act to gain or keep money; you value money. Students act to gain or keep good grades; they value good grades. Churchgoers act to gain or keep a relationship with "God"; they value that relationship. People act to develop or sustain fulfilling careers, to establish or maintain romantic relationships, to gain or keep freedom, and so on.

The key concept here is: *act*. Values are objects of *actions*. If someone *doesn't* act to achieve good grades, or to develop a fulfilling career, or to establish a relationship with God, then he doesn't value the thing in question. He might want the thing. He might dream about it. He might tell himself or others that he values it. He might feel that he *should* value it. But if he takes no action to gain or keep the thing, he doesn't truly value it. This is why, if a child leaves his bicycle out in the elements to rust, his parents properly say that he doesn't value the bicycle. A value is that which one acts to gain or keep.

Broadening our view, we can see that values pertain not only to people, but to *all* living things—and *only* to living things. Trees, tigers, and people take actions toward goals. Rocks, rivers, and hammers do not. Trees, for example, extend their roots into the ground and their branches and leaves toward the sky; they value minerals, water, and sunlight. Tigers hunt antelope and nap under trees; they value meat and shade. And people act to gain their values, such as food, education, and friendship. This pattern continues throughout the plant and animal kingdom: All living things take self-generated, goal-directed action.

Non-living things, on the other hand, take no such action. They can be moved, but they cannot act in the self-generated, goal-directed way that living things do. A rock remains still unless some outside force, such as a wave or a hammer, hits and moves it. A river flows, but its motion is not self-generated; water moves only by means of some outside force—in this case, the gravitational pull of the earth. And a hammer does not, by itself, smash rocks or drive nails; it does not generate its own action. Even a robot programmed to engage in some purposeful activity, such as vacuuming a carpet, does not take self-generated, goal-directed action. Rather, a robot acts only as it mechanically must, given that someone built and programmed it to act that way. In this case, the self-generated, goal-directed action is that of the programmer or the person using the robot.

Living things are unique in this respect: Only they take self-generated, goal-directed action. Only living things pursue values.

Why? Why do living things pursue values? What are values *for*?

At this point we can see, as Ayn Rand observed, that "the concept 'value' is not a primary; it presupposes an answer to the question: of value to *whom* and for *what*? It presupposes an entity capable of acting to achieve a goal in the face of an alternative."[6]

A tree faces the alternative of reaching water and sunlight—or not. A tiger faces the alternative of catching and keeping its prey—or not. And a person faces the alternative of achieving *his* goals—or not. To whom does the alternative matter? It matters to the organism taking the action. The objects a living thing acts to gain or keep are *its* values—values *to it.*

That answers the question: "to whom?" The question "for what?" remains.

What *difference* does it make whether an organism achieves its goals? What happens if it succeeds? What happens if it fails? What *ultimately* is at stake?

This question takes us to the very foundation of values, where we can see how rational morality is grounded in perceptual reality. As Rand observed, and as we can too:

> There is only one fundamental alternative in the universe: existence or non-existence—and it pertains to a single class of entities: to living organisms. The existence of inanimate matter is unconditional, the

> existence of life is not: it depends on a specific course of action. Matter is indestructible, it changes forms, but it cannot cease to exist. It is only a living organism that faces a constant alternative: the issue of life or death. Life is a process of self-sustaining and self-generated action. If an organism fails in that action, it dies; its chemical elements remain, but its life goes out of existence. It is only the concept of "Life" that makes the concept of "Value" possible.[7]

The reason why living things need values is: to *live*. The answer to the question "for *what*?" is: for *life*.

Life is *conditional*: If a living thing takes the actions and achieves the values necessary to remain alive, it remains alive. If, for some reason, it fails to take those actions or fails to achieve those values, it dies. And human beings are no exception to this principle. We need values for the same reason plants and other animals do: in order to sustain and further our life.

An organism's life is its *ultimate value*—the ultimate goal or end toward which its actions are the means. Consequently, an organism's life is its *standard* of value—the standard by reference to which all of its other values and actions can be objectively evaluated.[8]

Each form of life has its own specific needs as determined by its nature. And the requirements of a given organism's life constitute its standard of value. Nutrients, sunlight, and water are good for a tree—why? Because they serve its life. Meat, shade, and water are good for a tiger—why? Because they serve its life. And so on. For any given organism, the *good* is that which sustains or furthers its life, and the *bad* is that which harms or destroys it.[9]

Now, as human beings, we have *free will*, the ability to *choose* our values and actions, and this aspect of our nature adds a layer of complexity to the issue.

The ability to choose is what gives rise to the field of morality: Morality is the realm of *chosen* values. If we couldn't choose our values and actions, there would be no point in a science (or even conventions) dedicated to telling us which actions we should and shouldn't choose.[10]

Whereas other animals act automatically or instinctively to further their lives, people do not. A person *can* choose to act in ways that are contrary to the requirements of his life—as some people tragically do. For instance, a person can choose to consume harmful quantities of alcohol, opiates, or other drugs. Or a person can choose to do nothing but sit around and be unproductive, even though doing so will not advance or support his life. A person can even choose to commit suicide. Free will makes life-harming or even life-destroying action possible. Further, free will makes possible the choice to adopt a *morality* that is contrary to the requirements of human life, a morality that calls for people to sacrifice their life-serving values for the sake of "God" or others—as the morality of altruism does.[11]

So free will adds *significant* complexity to the question of values. But this complexity is substantially simplified by reference to a crucial observable fact: People don't *need* to take anti-life actions; nothing *in nature* necessitates or warrants such actions; there is *no reason* to act self-sacrificially.[12]

The fact that people can choose a course of action or even a code of values that is contrary to the requirements of their life does not change anything about the *objective standard* of value. Whatever anyone's choice, these facts remain: The only reason we *can* pursue values is because we are alive, and the only reason we *need* to pursue values is in order to live.

This observation-based, two-pronged principle is the key to grounding morality in reality, so it is worth emphasizing: Only life makes values *possible* (non-living things cannot pursue values), and only life makes values *necessary* (only living things need to pursue values). Put another way: You have to *be alive* in order to pursue values, and you have to pursue values in order to *stay alive.*

In accordance with this observation-based principle, the choices and actions that promote one's life are objectively good, and those that harm or destroy one's life are objectively bad.[13]

Observe, in this connection, that people generally regard matters of life and death as the most important matters of all. It is no coincidence that this commonsense idea corresponds to the very foundation of objective morality. The alternative of life or death—existence or non-existence—is the fundamental alternative that makes possible all other alternatives that matter. It is the basic alternative that gives rise to the possibility and need of values—and thus to the need of ideas such as *good* and *bad*, *right* and *wrong*, *matters* and *doesn't matter.* If it weren't for life and the goal of sustaining it, nothing would or could matter at all.

Ayn Rand's seminal discovery here is that life is the standard of value because life is the very reason why values exist. And *human* life—life in accordance with our nature as human beings—is the standard of *moral* value: the standard by reference to which we can determine which choices and actions are good or bad, right or wrong for human beings. As Rand put it, this observation-based standard encompasses "the terms, methods, conditions and goals required for the survival of a rational being through the whole of his lifespan—in all those aspects of existence which are open to his choice."[14]

As Rand specifies, the standard here pertains to the survival requirements of a *rational* being because that is what man is: a being who possesses—and survives by means of—the faculty of reason. That we possess the faculty of reason does not mean that we always or inevitably use that faculty. (Clearly, many people do not use reason regularly or even frequently.) Rather, it means that we can use reason if and when we *choose* to use it—and that using it is our basic means of living.[15] This makes our choice to use reason our basic life-serving virtue.

Using reason—observing reality, applying logic, identifying causal connections, and acting in accordance with the full context of one's knowledge—is objectively moral because doing so is essential to understanding reality and thus to living and prospering in reality. By contrast, refusing to use reason—turning away from facts, rejecting logic, pretending that causal connections are not real, and acting in disregard of what one knows to be true—is objectively immoral because doing so contradicts the requirements of human life.

We can see the consequences of rationality versus irrationality on every level of human life, from personal to social to political. Compare the life of Jeff Bezos to that of Bernie Madoff, or the culture of New Zealand to that of Saudi Arabia, or the political system of South Korea to that of North Korea. All else being equal, to the extent that individuals or societies proceed rationally, they progress, prosper, and flourish. To the extent that they proceed irrationally, they stagnate, suffer, and perish. These are causal relationships. Using reason sustains and advances human life; refusing to use it throttles and destroys human life. Thus, rationality—the commitment to use reason as a matter of principle in all areas of life—is the fundamental objective virtue.[16]

Likewise, being productive—creating goods or services for consumption or trade—is objectively moral because doing so is essential to human life and prosperity. Refusing to be productive is objectively immoral because it flies in the face of such facts. People who refuse to produce goods or services either die or exist parasitically on those who do produce them. Being productive is essential to human life and prosperity. Thus productiveness—the commitment to being productive as a matter of principle in life—is an objective virtue.[17]

Similarly, judging people rationally, in accordance with the available and relevant facts, and treating them accordingly, as they deserve to be treated, is objectively moral because doing so is essential to establishing and maintaining life-serving relationships—whether friendships, romantic relationships, business engagements, or political ties. Refusing to judge people rationally is objectively immoral because it is contrary to the requirements of life-serving relationships. People who fail to judge others rationally suffer life-throttling relationships and enable rights-violating political systems. Judging people rationally and treating them accordingly is vital; thus, justice, the commitment to doing so, is an objective virtue.[18]

The basic political principle supported by objective morality is worth emphasizing: Respecting people's rights—which means refraining from initiating physical force against people (whether direct force, such as a bullet to the head, or indirect force, such as fraud or extortion)—is objectively moral because people must be free from coercion in order to act in accordance with their own rational judgment and thus to live fully as human beings. A human life is a life guided by the judgment of one's own mind. Violating people's rights is objectively immoral—and properly illegal—because it stops people from acting on their judgment: their basic means of living. (For more on this point, see "Ayn Rand's Theory of Rights: The Moral Foundation of a Free Society.")[19]

The foregoing is merely a brief indication of how an objective standard of moral value along with corresponding moral principles and virtues are derived from and grounded in perceptual reality. But that much is sufficient to show that a secular, objective morality exists.

The controversial nature of this rational approach to morality escalates when we acknowledge the observable fact that human beings are *individuals*—each with his own body, his own mind, his own life.[20] This fact gives rise to the principle that each individual's *own* life is his *own* ultimate value. It means that each individual is morally an end in himself, not a means to the ends of others.[21] It means that the individual has neither a moral "duty" to sacrifice himself for the sake of "God" or others (as religion and altruism claim he does)—nor a moral "right" to sacrifice others for his own sake (as thugs and predators pretend they do).

In accordance with secular, observation-based, objective morality, neither self-sacrifice nor the sacrifice of others is moral, because, on principle, human sacrifice as such is *immoral*.

Human life does not require human sacrifice. It does not require people to give up their values for the sake of "God" or other people or some "greater good." Nor does it require people to attack others or to steal their belongings or to rape or otherwise assault them. People *can* live together rationally, civilly, peacefully. They can produce life-serving values and trade them with others by mutual consent and to mutual advantage. They can *refuse* to sacrifice themselves or others. And, if people commit to acting rationally, in a consistently life-serving manner, they can live and flourish in harmony with each other.

But, given the role of morality in human life—given the fact that the morality people accept as *true* substantially guides their choices and actions—in order for people to live in a consistently life-serving manner, they must embrace the morality that *advocates* living this way. They must embrace the secular, observation-based code of values we've been discussing: the morality Ayn Rand called "rational self-interest" or "rational egoism."

Rational egoism is not hedonism or subjectivism or predation. It does not call for acting on one's feelings, or doing whatever gives one pleasure, or sacrificing other people for one's alleged benefit. Those are caricatures of self-interest pushed by people who aim to discredit this morality but know that they can't unless they misrepresent it. Such caricatures are not logical arguments but straw men—and confessions of intellectual impotence, cowardice, or both.

Every thinking adult knows that the mere fact that someone "feels" like taking some action—or that he would get "pleasure" from taking it—or that he would get a "benefit" from taking it—does not mean that the action is in his self-interest. This is why rational parents strive to help their children learn the importance of *thinking*—observing reality and taking into account the available and relevant facts—before they act.

As rational parents know—and as rational egoism elaborates—there are proper and improper ways to treat one's feelings, to pursue pleasures, and to seek benefits. It is, of course, vital to acknowledge one's feelings, but one should always act in accordance with one's rational judgment—because feelings are not one's means of knowledge; reason is. It is good to pursue pleasures, but only if the pleasures are in concert with one's long-term self-interest—as judged by one's reasoning mind. And it is crucial to pursue benefits that will enhance one's life—but sacrificing or abusing others does not work toward that end; thinking, producing, trading, and engaging *rationally* with others does.

Again, the observations and integrations here are just an indication of the secular foundation and principles of objective morality. There is a great deal more to it—including the principle that the meaning of life is a function of one's chosen, life-serving purposes; the principle that for a virtue to be objective it must account for both the material and spiritual requirements of human life; and the principle that to make one's life the best it can be one must organize one's values hierarchically, according to their relative life-serving importance, and pursue them respectively. But the purpose of this short essay is not to examine every aspect of secular, objective morality. Its purpose is simply to show that such a morality exists and makes sense. (For a fleshed-out presentation of the foundations and principles of objective morality, see Ayn Rand's *The Virtue of Selfishness*, or my book *Loving Life: The Morality of Self-Interest and the Facts that Support It.*)[22]

People are free to continue claiming, "If there is no God, there is no objective morality." But they are not free to do so honestly. Ayn Rand's derivation of morality from reality is too clear and too accessible for anyone interested in this subject responsibly to neglect. If people think her reasoning is in error, they should point out where and how they think she erred. But to ignore the existence of Rand's ideas while asserting, "If there is no God, anything goes," is to engage in *evasion*: the refusal to think, the refusal to see, the refusal to know. Such evasion is akin to the Church's refusal to acknowledge Galileo's proof that the Earth orbits the Sun—except that those who evade Rand's proof have much more knowledge and, consequently, much less excuse.

It is time for everyone who cares about human life, happiness, and freedom to repudiate the nonsense that objective morality depends on God. Objective morality depends on *reason*—and, if we're willing to look, we can see that it does.

3

The Is-Altruism Dichotomy

A dichotomy is thwarting moral thought. Call it the "is-altruism dichotomy."

You've probably heard of the "is-ought dichotomy" or the "is-ought gap"—the idea that you cannot derive moral principles (principles regarding how people "ought" to act) from facts of reality (from what "is"). This idea originated with the Sophists of ancient Greece, who held that all moral views and values are subjective or mere opinions.[1] It was later popularized in terms of "is" and "ought" by the 18th century Scottish philosopher David Hume.[2] Today the idea is widely regarded as a fact beyond question. Outspoken scientist and atheist Sean Carroll sums up the view: "Attempts to derive ought from is are like attempts to reach an odd number by adding together even numbers. If someone claims that they've done it, you don't have to check their math; you know that they've made a mistake."[3]

The "is-ought dichotomy" is now affirmed, implicitly if not explicitly, by virtually all intellectuals; and taught, in some form or other, to practically all college students.[4] This is why so many educated people subscribe to moral relativism. If morality can't be grounded in reality, who's to say what's right?

Widespread acceptance of the "is-ought gap" not only breeds moral relativism; it also lends credence to claims that in order for objective morality to exist, there must be a divine lawmaker, a "God," who issues objective moral laws or commandments. "If moral standards are not rooted in God," says popular talk show host Dennis Prager, "they do not objectively exist. Good and evil are no more real than 'yummy' and 'yucky.' They are simply a matter of personal preference."[5]

But the idea that we can't derive moral standards from observable reality is demonstrably false. We certainly can—but we must first understand why man *needs* morality at all. If man needs morality, then the reason he needs it—the ultimate end it serves—logically sets the standard for determining the validity of moral principles and values. If man doesn't need morality, then he doesn't need it, and there is no point in discussing or even pondering the subject.

This is why the American philosopher Ayn Rand began her inquiry into ethics with the questions, "What are values? Why does man need them?" and "Why does man need a code of values?"[6] By looking at reality and pursuing answers to these and related questions, Rand discovered that values are the things one acts to gain or keep. For instance, we seek to gain or keep knowledge, food, wealth, relaxation, romance, and freedom. And she discovered that the ultimate reason we *need* values is *to live*—to sustain and further our lives. If we gain and keep values, we can live and prosper; if we fail to gain and keep them, we will suffer and die.

Rand discovered that *man's life*—meaning, the requirements of an individual's life and happiness on earth—is the standard of moral value: the ultimate standard against which we can judge good and bad, right and wrong, should and shouldn't. That which sustains and furthers man's life is the good; that which harms or destroys it is the evil. On this standard, moral virtues are the principled actions by means of which individuals pursue life-serving values.[7] For instance, looking at reality, thinking, producing goods or services, being honest, being just, trading value for value, advocating liberty, and the like are good because such actions serve and promote human life. Refusing to look at reality, refusing to think, acting parasitically, being dishonest, being unjust, engaging in theft, advocating tyranny, and the like are bad because such actions throttle or thwart human life. On the basis of this demonstrably true standard of value, Rand developed a secular, observation-based, objective morality—rational egoism—according to which each individual should pursue his own life-serving values and respect the rights of others to do the same. (For elaboration, see Rand's book *The Virtue of Selfishness: A New Concept of Egoism*, or my book *Loving Life: The Morality of Self-Interest and the Facts That Support It.*)

But Rand's rational, life-based approach to morality is far from the norm; very few people understand and embrace it. Even among those who have read her books, few recognize the virtue of selfishness. Why?

When people think about deriving morality from reality, what they usually have in mind is not "Why does man need values or morality?" This question *implies* that the purpose of morality, if it serves a purpose, is to enable man to gain or keep something; the question aims to discover a need-oriented standard of value—a standard that serves man's self-interest. If people were to ask and begin answering that question, they would soon see, as Rand did, that man's life is the standard of moral value, the ultimate reason he needs to gain or keep things; they would see that men need moral principles to guide their thought and action so they can live and prosper; and they would soon proceed to the next question: "What, in principle, are the requirements of man's life and happiness?"—which they would have no difficulty answering. They would simply look at reality and see that certain ideas, actions, and conditions are necessary for man's life, and that others are inimical to it, and they'd be on their way to grasping a fact-based morality. The problem is that when people approach the issue, they typically have in mind some form of *this* question: "How can the idea that you should selflessly serve others be derived from the facts of reality?" This common approach is a consequence of a fallacy Rand termed the fallacy of the frozen abstraction.

The fallacy of freezing an abstraction consists in substituting a particular conceptual concrete for the wider abstract class to which it belongs.[8] In the case at hand, it consists in substituting a specific morality, "altruism," for the general class "morality." This substitution is fallacious because, although altruism is a particular *type* of morality, it is not the *only* type of morality; it is not morality *as such*. The concept of "morality" is a broad category subsuming several kinds or codes of morality—altruism, egoism, hedonism, utilitarianism, and others. To substitute the concept of "altruism" for the concept of "morality" is to exclude from the broad category of "morality" all of the other moral codes that are properly included under it. Of course not every morality can be valid, but the question of which code is demonstrably true is a separate matter. Just as we do not treat "math" as the equivalent of "algebra" and thus exclude "geometry," "calculus," and other kinds of math from the field—just as we do not treat "religion" as the equivalent of "Christianity" and thus exclude Judaism, Islam, and other religions from the field—and just as we do not treat "government" as the equivalent of "theocracy" and thus exclude "democracy," "constitutional republicanism," and other types of government from the field—so we should not treat "morality" as the equivalent of "altruism." It is not.

When people freeze the broad abstraction of "morality" at the level of the narrower concrete of "altruism," they thereby preclude themselves from grounding morality in reality—because there simply are no facts to support the morality of altruism.[9] To see why, we must grasp the essence of the code.

Altruism is the idea that you should self-sacrificially serve others. Importantly, altruism does *not* hold that you should serve others in a way that results in a net gain on your part, as in selling a good or a service to a customer. Rather, altruism holds that you should serve others in a way that results in a net *loss* on your part, as in providing them with goods or services in exchange for nothing. Otherwise we'd have to regard Michael Dell as more altruistic than Mother Teresa, because he has served millions more people than she did. Dell, of course, serves people by employing them or selling them computers—that is, by exchanging value for value, an exchange in which both sides gain. Mother Teresa, on the other hand, served people by giving them her time and effort for nothing. That is a big difference. And it is an *essential* distinction regarding the nature of altruism. "Altruism," as New York University professor Thomas Nagel clarifies, entails "a willingness to act in consideration of the interests of other persons, without the need of ulterior motives"—"ulterior motives" meaning personal gains.[10]Princeton professor Peter Singer further clarifies, "to the extent that [people] are motivated by the prospect of obtaining a reward or avoiding a punishment, they are not acting altruistically."[11]Altruism calls not for pursuing gains, but for incurring losses; it calls for giving up your values (time, effort, wealth, etc.) in exchange for something less or for nothing at all. It calls for self-sacrifice.

A sacrifice is, as Ayn Rand put it, the surrender of a greater value for the sake of a lesser value or of a non-value.[12] If you spend your time selflessly serving strangers at a soup kitchen and thus forgo other uses of that time that would better serve your life and happiness—whether writing a novel that could launch your career, or snuggling with your lover, or camping with your friends, or exercising to maintain your health, or the like—then you are committing a sacrifice. You are giving up something more important to your life and happiness for the sake of something less important or unimportant. You are incurring a net loss. If, on the other hand, you spend your time maximally enhancing your life and happiness by always pursuing your life-serving values with respect to their relative importance toward that end, then you are not sacrificing; you are living selfishly.

Importantly, a choice or an exchange that results in a net gain cannot logically be construed as a sacrifice. Consider what such an equation would mean: "After due diligence and much negotiation, I paid the seller $90,000 dollars for the summer home of my dreams—what a sacrifice I made!" The reason that sounds wrong is that when I buy a house from a seller, both of us *profit* from the exchange. The house is more valuable to me than the money I exchange for it, and the money is more valuable to the seller than the house he exchanges for it. Such an exchange is not a sacrifice but a trade—a mutual gain.

Take another example: "I spent the day golfing with my best friend on our favorite course rather than golfing with a casual acquaintance on a lesser course. Just call me the sacrificial golfer!" Again, this is silly. If I forgo one outing in order to partake in a different outing because the latter is better for my life and happiness, I have not committed a sacrifice; I've upheld my hierarchy of values; I've steered my life in a self-interested manner; I've sought to maximize gains. To call this a "sacrifice" is to abuse words.

One more example: "Mother Teresa was clearly just out for personal gain. Look at all the sacrifices she made; imagine all the rewards she reaped. That's why the Church canonized her—because she was out to fill her life with goods and maximize her own happiness." Again, that just doesn't make sense—and Mother Teresa would have been the first to say so. Mother Teresa served people not for personal gain, but because she held that being moral consists in serving others self-sacrificially—serving others at a net loss—and because she wanted to be "moral" in accordance with that standard.

Gain-oriented actions and loss-oriented actions are essentially different kinds of actions, so we need different terms to denote them. We have perfectly clear terms for the kinds of actions that result in or are intended to result in net gains; they are "gains" or "trades" or "investments." And we have perfectly clear terms for the kinds of actions that result in or are intended to result in net losses; they are "losses" or "forfeits" or "sacrifices."

Altruism calls for you to surrender greater values for the sake of lesser values. It calls for you to *self-sacrificially* serve others—that is, to serve others at a net loss.

Now, given what altruism is, what facts of reality give rise to the need of it? None do. There is no such thing as a "need" to surrender greater values for the sake of lesser ones. Human life does not require self-sacrifice—or any kind of human sacrifice. Human life requires net gains in value, not net losses in value. It requires rational thought, productive effort, voluntary trade, political and economic freedom, and many other things; but it does not require sacrifice. The only thing that can be "accomplished" by means of sacrifice is suffering or death. And to "achieve" that end, a person need not do anything; he can just stop acting and he'll be miserable or expire in short order.

In contrast, what facts of reality give rise to the principle that people should pursue values and achieve net gains? When we look around, we see plenty of facts that give rise to this principle.

Look at reality and your life. If you want to live fully and happily, you *must* pursue life-serving values—and you must refuse to surrender those that are more important for the sake of those that are less important. For instance, you must choose life-serving career goals and work to achieve them; you must engage in recreational and leisure activities that bring you joy; you must establish and maintain relationships conducive to your life and happiness; you must work to establish and maintain liberty so that you can act on your judgment. To the extent that you take such actions and succeed, you can live and prosper; to the extent that you don't, you can't.

Self-interested action is essential to a life of happiness, self-sacrificial action is detrimental to it, and reality is full of facts to support these truths.

If moral principles or "oughts" are ideas to guide our choices and actions in service of our life and happiness (and they are), then we certainly *can* derive them from the facts of reality. And we not only can; we *must*—that is, *if* we want to live and prosper.

The reason contemporary philosophers and intellectuals—including "New Atheists" and "secular humanists"—have been unable to bridge the "is-ought gap" is that they have not been trying to derive morality from reality. Rather, they have been trying to derive *altruism* from reality—and there simply are no facts that give rise to the need of self-sacrifice.

The dichotomy at hand is not between reality and morality, but between reality and altruism. You can't derive altruism from facts. And thank goodness for that.

4

Atlas Shrugged and Ayn Rand's Morality of Egoism

Because of its seemingly prophetic nature with respect to current events, Ayn Rand's 1957 novel *Atlas Shrugged* is receiving more attention and selling at greater volume today than it did when it was first published fifty-five years ago. That's a good thing, because the ideas set forth in *Atlas* are crucial to personal happiness, social harmony, and political freedom.

Atlas Shrugged is first and foremost a brilliant suspense story about a man who said he would stop the motor of the world and did. But the book is much more than a great novel. Integrated into the story is a revolutionary philosophy—a philosophy not for pie-in-the-sky debates or academic word games or preparing for an "afterlife," but for understanding reality, achieving values, and living on earth.

Rand's philosophy, which she named Objectivism, includes a view of the nature of reality, of man's means of knowledge, of man's nature and means of survival, of a proper morality, of a

---

Author's note: This is an expanded version of a talk I've delivered on various college campuses over the past several years.

proper social system, and of the nature and value of art. It is a comprehensive philosophy, which, after writing *Atlas Shrugged*, Rand elaborated in several nonfiction books. But it all came together initially in *Atlas*, in which Rand dramatized her philosophy—along with the ideas that oppose it.

While writing *Atlas*, Rand made a journal entry in which she said, "My most important job is the formulation of a *rational morality of and for man, of and for his life, of and for this earth*."[1] She proceeded to formulate just such a morality, and to show what it means in practice.

Tonight, we're going to focus on the morality presented in *Atlas Shrugged*, but I want to do so without spoiling the novel for those of you who haven't yet read it. And since it is impossible to say much of substance about *Atlas* without giving away key elements of its plot and the mystery of the novel, I'm going to limit my discussion of the book to a brief indication of its plot—without giving away anything pivotal—after which I'll discuss Rand's morality of egoism directly.

Atlas Shrugged is a story about a future world in which the entire globe, with the exception of America, has fallen under the rule of various "People's States" or dictatorships. America, the only country that is not yet fully socialized, is sliding rapidly in that direction, as it increasingly accepts the ideas that lead to dictatorship, ideas such as self-sacrifice is noble, self-interest is evil, and greedy producers and businessmen have a moral obligation to serve the "greater good" of society.

Given this cultural climate, the economy becomes increasingly regulated by the government, and the country slides further and further into economic chaos: Factories shut down, trains stop running, businesses close their doors, people starve—just what you would expect if the U.S. government started acting like the government of the USSR.

But then, something strange starts happening. America's top producers—various scientists, inventors, businessmen, and artists—start to disappear. One by one, they simply vanish. And no one knows where they've gone or why.

Consequently, the supply of goods and services—from scientific discoveries to copper to wheat to automobiles to oil to medicine to entertainment—reduces to a trickle and eventually comes to a halt. Life as Americans once knew it ceases to exist. The country is in ruins.

Where did the producers go and why? Were they killed? Were they kidnapped? Do they return? How is this resolved?

Read the book. You'll be riveted.

As I said, I don't want to give away the story, but I will mention its theme. The theme of *Atlas Shrugged*is the role of the mind in man's existence. The novel dramatizes the fact that the reasoning mind is the basic source of the values on which human life depends. And this is not only the theme of *Atlas*; it is also the essence of Rand's philosophy of Objectivism: Reason—the faculty that operates by means of observation, concepts, and logic—is the source of all knowledge, values, and prosperity.

In this same vein, the theme of my talk tonight is the role of the mind—specifically *your* mind—in understanding, evaluating, and embracing a moral code.

Suppose you are offered two moral codes from which to choose—and whichever one you choose, you have to live by it for the rest of your life. The first code tells you that your life is supremely important—that it is properly the single most important thing in the world to you. This code says that you should live a wonderful, joy-filled life, and it provides an abundance of guidance about how to do so: how to make your life great; how to choose your goals, organize your values, and prioritize the things that are important to you; how to succeed in school, in friendships, and in romance; how to choose a career that you'll love and how to succeed in it. And so on. In short, this first moral code provides you guidance for achieving a lifetime of happiness and prosperity.

The second moral code offers an entirely different kind of guidance. It tells you *not* that you should live a wonderful life, *not* that you should pursue and achieve your goals and values—but, rather, that your life is *unimportant*, that you should *sacrifice* your values, that you should give them up for the "sake" of others, that you should abandon the pursuit of personal happiness and accept the kind of "life" that results from doing so. That's it. That's the guidance provided by the second code.

All else being equal, which moral code would you choose—and why?

I suspect that, on serious reflection, you would choose the first code. I further suspect that your reasoning would be something on the order of: "We're talking about my *life* here. If it's true that embracing the first code will make my life wonderful, and embracing the second will make it miserable, then this is a no-brainer."

I think that's good reasoning. Let's see if it holds up under scrutiny as we flesh out the respective natures and implications of these two codes.

The first code is Rand's morality of rational egoism, which lies at the heart of *Atlas Shrugged* and is the centerpiece of Objectivism. The second code is the traditional ethics of altruism—which is the cause of all the trouble in *Atlas Shrugged* and is the ethics on which we all were raised. In order to be clear about what Rand's egoism is, I want to compare and contrast it with altruism. This will serve to highlight the value of Rand's ideas and help to dispel potential misconceptions about her views. It will also show how destructive altruism is and why we desperately need to replace it with rational egoism—both personally and culturally. (I will be using the terms "egoism" and "rational egoism" interchangeably for reasons that will become clear as we proceed.)

Let me stress that I cannot present the whole of Rand's morality in one evening—that would be impossible. What I'm going to do is just indicate its *essence*, by discussing a few of its key principles. My aim is to show you that there is something enormously important here—something important to *your life and happiness*—and to inspire you to look further into the subject on your own.

To begin, observe that each of you brought a morality with you tonight. It is right there in your head—whether you are conscious of it or not. Each of you has a set of ideas about what is good and bad, right and wrong—about what you should and shouldn't do. And you refer to these ideas, implicitly or explicitly, when making choices and taking actions in your daily life. Should I study for the test, or cheat on it, or not worry about it? What career should I choose—and how should I choose it? Is environmentalism a good movement or a bad one? What should I do this weekend? How should I spend my time? Whom should I befriend? Whom can I trust? Is homosexuality wrong? Does a fetus have rights? What is the proper way to deal with terrorists?

The answers one gives to such questions depend on one's morality. This is what a morality is: a set of ideas and principles to guide one's choices, evaluations, and actions.

Because as human beings we *have to* make choices—because we have free will—a morality of some kind is unavoidable to us. Morality is truly inescapable. Our only choice in this regard is whether we acquire our morality through conscious deliberation—or by default, through social osmosis.

If we acquire our morality by default, we will most likely accept the dominant morality in the culture today: *altruism*—the idea that being moral consists in being *selfless*. "Don't be selfish!"—"Put others first!"—"It is more blessed to give than to receive."—"Ask not what your country can do for you; ask what you can do for your country."—"Volunteer to serve in your community."—"Sacrifice for the greater good." And so on.

This is the morality that surrounded all of us growing up—and that still surrounds us today. It is the morality taught in church, synagogue, and school—offered in books, movies, and on TV—and encouraged by most parents.

Interestingly, however, although our culture is steeped in this morality, the actual meaning of altruism, in the minds of most people, is quite vague. Is a doctor acting altruistically when he cares for his patients? Or is he seeking to *gain* from doing so? Are parents being altruistic when they pay for their children's education? Or is it in their best interest to do so? Are American soldiers acting altruistically when they defend our freedom? Or is defending our freedom in their self-interest? Are you acting altruistically when you throw a birthday party for your best friend? Or do you do so because he or she is a great value *to you*—and thus, something is in it *for you*?

What exactly is the difference between self-*less* action and self-*interested* action? What is the difference between altruism and egoism?

To understand how each differs from the other, we need to understand the basic theory of each code and what each calls for in practice. To begin clarifying this issue, let us turn first to altruism.

Altruism is the morality that holds self-sacrificial service as the standard of moral value and as the sole justification for one's existence. Here, in the words of altruistic philosopher W. G. Maclagan, is the basic principle: According to altruism, "the moral importance of being alive lies in its constituting the condition of our ability to serve ends that are not reducible to our personal satisfactions."[2] This means that the moral importance of your life corresponds to your acts of *selflessness*—acts that do not satisfy your personal needs. Insofar as you do *not* act selflessly, your life has *no* moral significance. Quoting Maclagan again, altruism holds that we have "a duty to relieve the stress and promote the happiness of our fellows. . . . [We] should discount altogether [our] own pleasure or happiness as such when . . . deciding what course of action to pursue. . . . [Our] own happiness is, as such, a matter of no moral concern to [us] whatsoever."[3]

Ayn Rand was not exaggerating when she said, "The basic principle of altruism is that man has no right to exist for his own sake, that service to others is the only justification of his existence, and that self-sacrifice is his highest moral duty, virtue, and value."[4] That *is* the theoretical meaning of altruism. And the altruistic philosophers know it—and state it forthrightly. (We'll hear from more of them a little later.)

Now, what does altruism mean in practice? Suppose a person accepts altruism as true and strives to practice it consistently. What will become of his life?

A widely-used college philosophy text gives us a good indication. As I read this passage, bear in mind that this is not someone speaking for or against altruism. This is just a textbook writer's depiction of what altruism means in practice.

> A *pure* altruist doesn't consider her own welfare at all but only that of others. If she had a choice between an action that would produce a great benefit for herself (such as enabling her to go to college) and an action that would produce no benefit for herself but a small benefit for someone else (such as enabling him to go to a concert this evening), she should do the second. She should be *selfless*,

> considering herself not at all: she should face death rather than subject another person to a minor discomfort. She is committed to serving others only and to pass up any benefits to herself.[5]

That illustrates the practical meaning of altruism—and indicates why no one practices it consistently.

Observe, however, that whether practiced consistently or inconsistently, the basic *principle* of altruism remains the same: The only moral justification of your existence is self-sacrificial service to others. That some people subscribe to altruism but fail to uphold it consistently does not make their moral code different in *kind* from that of a person who practices it consistently; the difference is only one of *degree*. The consistent altruist is acting with a bizarre form of "integrity"—the kind of integrity that leads to his suffering and death. The inconsistent altruist is acting with plain-old hypocrisy—albeit a necessary hypocrisy given his moral code.

And not only is the altruist's *morality* the same in kind; the *consequences* of accepting it are the same in kind, too. To the extent that a person acts selflessly, he thereby thwarts his life and happiness. He might not die because of it, but he certainly will not live fully; he will not make the most of his life; he will not achieve the kind of happiness that is possible to him.

Have *you* accepted the principle of altruism? If so, how is it affecting your life?

Have you ever done something for the sake of others—at the expense of what you really thought was best for your *own* life? For instance: Have you ever accepted an invitation to dine with someone whose company you do not enjoy—because you didn't want to hurt his or her feelings? Have you ever skipped an event—such as a ski trip or a weekend at the beach with your friends—in order to spend time with family members you'd really rather not see? Have you ever remained in a relationship that you know is not in your best interest—because you think that he or she couldn't handle the breakup?

Conversely, have you ever felt guilty for *not* sacrificing for others? Have you ever felt ashamed for doing something that was in your own best interest? For instance, have you felt guilty for not giving change to a beggar on a street corner? Or guilty for pursuing a degree in business or art or something you love—rather than doing something allegedly "noble," such as joining the Peace Corps?

These are just some of the consequences of accepting the morality of altruism.

Altruism is not good for your life: If you practice it consistently, it leads to death. That's what Jesus did. If you accept it and practice it inconsistently, it retards your life and leads to guilt. This is what most altruists do.

Rational egoism, as the name suggests, and as we will see, *is* good for your life. It says that you should *pursue* your life-serving values and should *not* sacrifice yourself for the sake of others. Practiced consistently, it leads to a life of happiness. Practiced inconsistently—well, *why* be inconsistent here? Why *not* live a life of happiness? Why sacrifice *at all*? What *reason* is there to do so? (We will address the profound lack of an answer to this question later.)

At this point, we can begin to see why Rand called altruism "The Morality of Death." To fully grasp why it is the morality of death, however, we must understand that the essence of altruism is not "serving others" but *self-sacrifice.* So I want to reiterate this point with emphasis.

Altruism does *not* call merely for "serving others"; it calls for *self-sacrificially* serving others. Otherwise, Michael Dell would have to be considered more altruistic than Mother Teresa. Why? Because Michael Dell serves millions more people than Mother Teresa ever did.

There is a difference, of course, in the way he serves people. Whereas Mother Teresa "served" people by exchanging her time and effort for *nothing*, Michael Dell serves people by *trading* with them—by exchanging value for value to mutual advantage—an exchange in which both sides *gain*.

Trading value for value is not the same thing as *giving up* values for nothing. There is a black-and-white difference between pursuing values and giving them up—between achieving values and relinquishing them—between exchanging a *lesser* value for a *greater* one—and vice versa.

In an effort to make their creed seem more palatable, pushers of altruism will try to blur this distinction in your mind. It is important not to let them get away with it. Don't be duped!

Altruists claim, for instance, that parents "sacrifice" when they pay for their children to attend college. But this is ridiculous: Presumably, parents value their children's education more than they value the money they spend on it. If so, then the sacrifice would be for them to forgo their children's education and spend the money on a lesser value—such as a Ferrari.

Altruists also claim that romantic love requires "sacrifices." But this is ridiculous, too: "Honey, I'd really rather be with another woman, but here I am sacrificially spending my time with you." Or: "I'd really rather have spent this money on a new set of golf clubs, but instead I sacrificially bought you this necklace for your birthday." Or: "It's our anniversary—so I'm fixing you your favorite dish for a candlelit dinner—even though I'd rather be playing poker with the guys."

Is that love? Only if love is sacrificial.

Altruists also claim that American soldiers sacrifice by serving in the military. Not so. Our non-drafted soldiers serve for a number of self-interested reasons. Here are three: (1) They serve for the same reason that the Founding Fathers formed this country—because they value liberty, because they realize that liberty is a requirement of human life, which is the reason why Patrick Henry ended his famous speech with "Give me Liberty or give me Death!" His was not an ode to sacrifice; it was an ode to life, liberty, and the pursuit of happiness. (2) Our soldiers serve in exchange for payment and education—which are clearly in their self-interest. (3) They serve because they are fascinated by military science and want to make a career of it—another selfish motive.

Do some of these soldiers die in battle? Unfortunately, yes. Theirs is a dangerous job. But American soldiers don't *willfully* give up their lives: They don't walk out on the battlefield and say, "Shoot me!" Nor do they strap bombs to their bodies and detonate themselves in enemy camps. On the contrary, they do everything they can to beat the enemy, win the war, and *remain alive*—even when the Bush and Obama administrations tie their hands with altruistic restrictions on how they can fight.

The point is that a sacrifice is not "any choice or action that precludes some other choice or action." A sacrifice is not "any old exchange." A sacrifice is, as Rand put it, "the surrender of a greater value for the sake of a lesser one or of a non-value."[6]

Whether or not one is committing a sacrifice depends on what is *more* important and what is *less*important to one's life. To make this determination, of course, one must know the relative importance of one's values in regard to one's life. But if one does establish this hierarchy, one *can* proceed non-sacrificially—and consistently so.

For example, if you know that your education is more important to your life than is, say, a night on the town with your friends, then if you stay home in order to study for a crucial exam—rather than going out with your buddies—that is not a sacrifice. The sacrifice would be to hit the town and botch the exam.

Life requires that we regularly forgo lesser values for the sake of greater ones. But these are *gains*, not sacrifices. A sacrifice consists in giving up something that is *more* important for the sake of something that is *less* important; thus, it results in a net loss.

Altruism, the morality of self-sacrifice, is the morality of *personal loss*—and it does not countenance personal gain. This is not a caricature of altruism; it is the *essence* of the morality. As arch-altruist Peter Singer (the famed utilitarian philosopher at Princeton University) explains, "to the extent that [people] are motivated by the prospect of obtaining a reward or avoiding a punishment, they are not acting altruistically. . . ."[7] Arch-altruist Thomas Nagel (a philosophy professor at New York University) concurs: Altruism entails "a willingness to act in consideration of the interests of other persons, without the need of ulterior motives"—"ulterior motives" meaning, of course, personal gains.[8]

To understand the difference between egoistic action and altruistic action, we must grasp the difference between a trade and a sacrifice—between a gain and a loss—and we must not allow altruists to blur this distinction in our mind. Egoism, as we will see, calls for personal gains. Altruism, as we have seen, calls for personal losses.

Now, despite its destructive nature, altruism is accepted to some extent by almost everyone today. Of course, no one upholds it *consistently*—at least not for long. Rather, most people accept it as true—and then cheat on it.

All the major religions—Christianity, Judaism, Islam—advocate altruism; their holy books demand it. All so-called "secular humanist" philosophies—utilitarianism, postmodernism, egalitarianism—call for altruism as well. (Note that "secular humanists" do not call themselves "secular egoists" or "secular individualists.")

"Alter" is Latin for "other"; "altruism" means "other-ism"; it holds that you should sacrifice for others. From the Christian, Jewish, and Muslim points of view, the significant "others" are "God" and "the poor"; in the Old Testament, for instance, God says: "I command you to be openhanded toward your brothers and toward the poor and needy in your land" (Deuteronomy 15:11). From the utilitarian point of view, the "other" is "everyone in general"; the utilitarian principle is "the greatest good for the greatest number." From the postmodern and egalitarian points of view, the "other" is anyone with less wealth or opportunity than you have; in other words, the better off you are, the more you should sacrifice for others—the worse off you are, the more others should sacrifice for you.

Sacrifice. Sacrifice. Sacrifice. Everyone believes it is the moral thing to do. And no philosopher has been willing to challenge this idea.

Except Ayn Rand:

> [T]here is one word—a single word—which can blast the morality of altruism out of existence and which it cannot withstand—the word: "*Why?*" *Why* must man live for the sake of others? *Why* must he be a sacrificial animal? *Why* is that the good? There is no earthly reason for it—and, ladies and gentlemen, in the whole history of philosophy no *earthly*reason has ever been given.[9]

On examination, this is true. No reason has ever been given as to why people should sacrifice for others. Of course, *alleged* reasons have been given, but not legitimate ones. So let's consider the alleged reasons—of which there are approximately six—each of which involves a logical fallacy.

1. *"You should sacrifice because God (or some other voice from another dimension) says so."* This is not a reason—certainly not

an earthly one. At best, it is an appeal to authority—that is, to the "authorities" who claim to speak for God. Just because a preacher or a book makes a claim does not mean the claim is true. The Bible claims, among other things, that a bush spoke. More fundamentally, this non-reason is an arbitrary claim because there is no evidence for the existence of a god. But even those who believe in a god can recognize the fallacy of appealing to an authority.

2. *"You should sacrifice because that's the general consensus."* This is not a reason but an appeal to the masses. Matters of truth and morality are not determined by consensus. That slavery should be legal used to be the general consensus in America, and is still the consensus in parts of Africa. That did not and does not make it so. Nor does consensus legitimize the notion that you or anyone else should sacrifice or be sacrificed.

3. *"You should sacrifice because other people need the benefit of your sacrifice."* This is an appeal to pity. Even if other people did need the benefit of your sacrifice, it would not follow that this is a reason to sacrifice. More importantly, however, the notion that people need the benefit of your sacrifice is false. What people need is to produce values and to trade them with others who produce values. And to do so, they and others must be *free* to produce and trade according to their own judgment. This, not human sacrifice, is what human life requires. (I'll touch on the relationship between freedom and egoism a little later.)

4. *"You should sacrifice because if you don't, you will be beaten, or fined, or thrown in jail, or in some other way physically assaulted."* The threat of force is not a reason; it is the opposite of a reason. If the force wielders could offer a reason why you should sacrifice, then they would not have to use force; they could use persuasion instead of coercion.

5. *"You should sacrifice because, well, when you grow up or wise up you'll see that you should."* This is not a reason, but

a personal attack and an insult. It says, in effect, "If you don't see the virtue of sacrifice, then you're childish or stupid"—as if demanding a reason in support of a moral conviction could indicate a lack of maturity or intelligence.

6. *"You should sacrifice because only a miscreant or a scoundrel would challenge this established fact."* This kind of claim assumes that you regard others' opinions of you as more important than your own judgment of truth. It is also an example of what Ayn Rand called "The Argument from Intimidation": the attempt to substitute psychological pressure for rational argument. Like the personal attack, it is an attempt to avoid having to present a rational case for a position for which no rational case can be made.

That's it. Such are the "reasons" offered in support of the claim that you should sacrifice. Don't take my word for it; ask around. Ask your philosophy professors. Ask a priest or rabbi. You will find that all the "reasons" offered are variants of these—each of which, so far from being a "reason," is a textbook logical fallacy. (Most even have fancy Latin names.)

Ayn Rand demanded *reasons* for her convictions. So should we.

She set out to discover a *rational* morality—one based on observable facts and logic. Rather than starting with the question "Which of the existing codes of value should I accept?"—she began with the question, "What are values and why does man need them?" This question pointed her away from the established views—and toward the facts of reality.

Looking at reality, Rand observed that a value is that which one acts to gain or keep. You can see the truth of this in your own life: You act to gain and keep money; you value it. You act to gain and keep good grades; you value them. You act to choose and develop a fulfilling career. You seek to meet the right guy or girl and build a wonderful relationship. And so on.

Looking at reality, Rand also saw that only living organisms take self-generated, goal-directed action. Trees, tigers, and people take actions toward goals. Rocks, rivers, and hammers do not. Trees, for example, extend their roots into the ground and their branches and leaves toward the sky; they value nutrients and sunlight. Tigers hunt antelope, and nap under trees; they value food and shade. And people act to gain *their* values, such as nutrition, education, a career, romance, and so on.

Further, Rand saw that the ultimate reason living organisms take such actions is to further their *life*. She discovered that an organism's life is its ultimate goal and standard of value—and that *man's* life is the standard of *moral* value: the standard by which one judges what is good and what is evil. Man's life—meaning: that which is required to sustain and further the life of a human being—constitutes the standard of moral value.

Now, the validation of the principle that life is the standard of value has a number of aspects, and we don't have time to consider all of them tonight. For our purposes here, I want to focus briefly on just a few.

By pursuing the question "Why does man need values?"—Ayn Rand kept her thinking *fact-oriented*. If man needs values, then the *reason* he needs them will go a long way toward establishing which values are legitimate and which are not. If man doesn't need values, well, then, he doesn't need them—and there is no point in pursuing the issue at all. What Rand discovered is that man *does* need values—and the reason he needs them is in order to *live*. *Life*, she discovered, is the ultimate goal of our actions; life is the final end toward which all our other values are properly the means.

Granted, because we have free will we can take antilife actions—and, as we have seen, altruism senselessly calls for us to do just that. But the point is that we don't *need* to take antilife actions, unless we want to die—in which case, we don't really need to take any action at all. We don't need to do anything in order to die; if that's what we want, we can simply stop acting altogether and we will soon wither away.

If we want to live, however, we must pursue life-serving values—and we must do so by choice.

Free will enables us to choose our values. This is what gives rise to the field of morality. Morality *is* the realm of chosen values. But whatever our choices, these facts remain: The only reason we *can* pursue values is because we are alive, and the only reason we *need* to pursue values is in order to live.

This two-pronged principle of Rand's philosophy is essential to understanding how the Objectivist morality is grounded in the immutable facts of reality: (1) Only life makes values *possible*—since nonliving things cannot pursue values; and (2) only life makes values *necessary*—since only living things need to pursue values.

Observing reality, we can see that this is true: A rock doesn't have values. It *can't* act to gain or keep things; it just stays still—unless some outside force, such as a wave or a hammer, hits and moves it. And it doesn't *need* to gain or keep things, because its continued existence is *unconditional.* A rock can change forms—for instance, it can be crushed and turned to sand, or melted and turned to liquid—but it cannot go out of existence. The continued existence of a *living organism*, however, is *conditional*—and this is what gives rise to the possibility and need of values. A tree must achieve certain ends—or else it will die. Its chemical elements will remain, but its life will go out of existence. A tiger must achieve certain ends, too, or it will meet the same fate. And a person—if he is to remain alive—must achieve certain ends as well.

The Objectivist ethics—recognizing all of this—holds *human life* as the standard of moral value. It holds that acting in accordance with the requirements of human life is moral, and acting in contradiction to those requirements is immoral. It is a fact-based, black-and-white ethics.

Now, combining the principle that human life is the standard of moral value with the observable fact that people are individuals—each with his *own* body, his *own* mind, his *own* life—we reach another principle of the Objectivist ethics: Each individual's *own* life is his *own* ultimate value. This means that each individual is *morally* an end in himself—not a means to the ends of others. Accordingly, he has no moral "duty" to sacrifice himself for the sake of others. Nor does he have a moral "right" to sacrifice others for his own sake. On principle, neither self-sacrifice nor the sacrifice of others is moral, because, on principle, *human sacrifice as such is immoral.*

Human life does not require people to sacrifice themselves for the sake of others; nor does it require people to sacrifice others for their own sake. Human life simply does not require human sacrifice; people *can* live without giving up their minds, their values, their lives; people *can* live without killing, beating, robbing, or defrauding one another.

Moreover, human sacrifice cannot promote human life and happiness; it can lead only to suffering and death. If people want to live and be happy they must neither sacrifice themselves nor sacrifice others; rather, they must pursue life-serving values and respect the rights of others to do the same. And, given the role of morality in human life, in order to do so, they must accept the morality that *advocates*doing so.

In a sentence, the Objectivist ethics holds that human sacrifice is immoral—and that each person should pursue his own life-serving values and respect the rights of others to do the same. This is the basic principle of rational egoism. And the reason it sounds so good is because it *is* good; it is *right*; it is *true*. This principle is derived from the observable facts of reality and the demonstrable requirements of human life. Where else could valid moral principles come from? And what other purpose could they serve?

We can now see why Ayn Rand said, "The purpose of morality is to teach you, not to suffer and die, but to enjoy yourself and live." Morality, properly conceived, is not a hindrance to a life of happiness; rather, it is the *means* to such a life.

So let us turn to the question of *how* to enjoy yourself and live. If that is the right thing to do, then what—according to the Objectivist ethics—is the means to that end?

First and foremost, in order to live and achieve happiness, we have to use *reason*. Hence the technically redundant word "rational" in "rational egoism." Reason is our means of understanding the world, ourselves, and our needs. It is the faculty that operates by means of perceptual observation and conceptual abstraction—by means of our five senses and our ability to think logically, to make causal connections, and to form principles.

It is by means of reason that we identify what things are, what properties they have, and how we can use them for our life-serving purposes. For example, it is by the use of reason that we learn about plants, soil, the principles of agriculture, and how to produce food. It is by means of reason that we learn about wool, silk, and how to make looms and produce clothing. It is by means of reason that we learn the principles of chemistry and biology and how to produce medicine and perform surgery; the principles of engineering and how to build homes and skyscrapers; the principles of aerodynamics and how to make and fly jumbo jets; the principles of physics and how to produce and control nuclear energy. And so on.

On a more personal level, it is by means of reason that we are able to develop fulfilling careers, to engage in rewarding hobbies, and to establish and maintain good friendships. And it is by means of reason that we are able to achieve success in romance.

Since this last is perhaps less obvious than the others, let's focus on it for a minute.

To establish and maintain a good romantic relationship, you have to take into account all the relevant facts pertaining to that goal. To begin with, you have to know what kind of relationship will actually be good for your life; you were not born with this knowledge, nor do you gain it automatically. To acquire it, you have to observe reality and think logically. Further, you have to find someone who suits your needs and lives up to your standards. To do so, you have to judge peoples' characters and qualities accurately—which requires reason. Once found, you have to treat the person justly—as he or she deserves to be treated. To do this, you have to understand and apply the principle of justice (which we will discuss shortly). Your means of understanding and applying it is reason.

To succeed in romance, you have to discover and act in accordance with a lot of facts and principles. You must think and act rationally. If you choose a lover irrationally, or treat your lover irrationally, then your love life will be doomed. I'm sure you all know of people who approach relationships irrationally—and what the results are.

The Objectivist ethics recognizes that reason is our basic means of living and achieving happiness. Thus, it upholds reason as our guide in *all* areas of life: material, spiritual, personal, social, sexual, professional, recreational—you name it.

Now, what about emotions? Where do they fit into the picture?

The Objectivist ethics recognizes and upholds the crucial role of emotions in human life and happiness. Emotions are our psychological means of enjoying life—which is the whole purpose of living. But, toward that end, it is important to treat emotions for what they *are* and not to expect them to be what they are *not*.

What exactly are emotions? They are automatic consequences of our *value judgments*. They arise from our *evaluations* of the things, people, and events in our lives. For instance, if you apply for a job that you consider ideal for your career path, and you get it, you will experience positive, joyful emotions. If you don't get it, you will experience feelings of frustration or disappointment. Similarly, if you have not seen your good friend for a long time and you run into him in a restaurant, you will be thrilled to see him. If, however, he informs you that he has joined the Church of Scientology, you will become highly upset. If he later tells you he was kidding, you will feel somewhat relieved. Likewise, if your favorite team wins a big game, you will react one way. If your team loses, you will react another way—especially if you bet a lot of money on the game.

Your emotions reflect what is important to you; they are, as Rand put it, "lightning-like estimates of the things around you, calculated according to your values." As such, they are *crucial* to your life. If you did not experience the emotion of desire, you would have no motivation to take any actions at all—and you would soon die. If you never experienced joy, you would have no reason to remain alive; a life devoid of joy is not a life worth living. We *need* emotions.

But emotions are not our means of knowledge. They cannot tell us which berries are edible or how to build a hut, how to perform heart surgery or how to make an iPod, who is honest or who has a right to do what, what to do about terrorism or what will make us happy. Only reason can tell us such things.

Thus, rational egoism holds that we should respect each of

our mental faculties for what it *is*. Unlike emotionalist moralities—which treat emotions as if they can tell us what is true and what is good and what is right—the Objectivist morality recognizes emotions for exactly what they are and treats them accordingly. To expect emotions to be what they are not—or to do what they cannot—is to misuse them. Just as we do not call child-abusers "pro-child," so we should not call emotion-abusers "pro-emotion." They are not.

The Objectivist ethics *is* pro-emotion—and it is the only moral code that is so. It is both 100 percent pro-reason—and 100 percent pro-emotion. It calls for the proper use of each mental faculty at all times on the grounds that human life and happiness *depend* on their proper use.

Reason is our only means of knowledge—and thus our basic means of living. Emotions are automatic consequences of our value judgments—and thus our psychological means of enjoying life. Properly understood, reason and emotions are not warring aspects of human nature; rather, they are a harmonious, life-serving team.

The Objectivist ethics holds that you should pursue your life-serving values with the *whole* of your life in mind, including all of your needs—physical, intellectual, and emotional—over your entire life span. Your basic means of doing so is reason.

Thus, egoism does *not* call for "doing whatever one pleases" or "doing whatever one feels like doing" or "stabbing others in the back to get what one wants." Those are caricatures of egoism perpetrated by pushers of altruism who seek to equate egoism with hedonism, subjectivism, and predation. Again, don't be duped! Egoism is *not* hedonism; it does not say: "Do whatever gives you *pleasure* regardless of its effects on your life." Egoism is *not* subjectivism; it does not say: "Do whatever you *feel* like doing regardless of the consequences." And egoism is *not* predation;

it not only denies that you *should* achieve values by abusing others; it fundamentally denies that you even *can* achieve life-serving values through dishonesty, injustice, or coercion.

Egoism does not hold pleasure or feelings or conquest as the standard of value. It holds *life* as the standard of value—and reason as your basic means of living. Thus, an egoist strives always to act in his long-term best interest—as judged by his use of reason. In other words, an egoist is *rationally goal-oriented*, which brings us to another key aspect of Rand's morality: the value of *purpose*.

A purpose is a conscious, intentional goal. A person acting purposefully is *after* something—as against meandering or wandering aimlessly. The rational pursuit of life-serving goals is the essence of good living; purpose is a hallmark of self-interest.

If we want to make the most of our days and years—if we want to be *fully* selfish—we have to be consciously goal-directed in every area of our life where choice applies. For instance, we have to choose a career that we will love. We have to think rationally about how to succeed in it. We need to plan long range and work hard to achieve excellence and happiness in our chosen field. We also have to choose and pursue interesting hobbies and recreational activities that will bring us great joy—whether making music or riding horses or surfing or blogging or the like. And, as mentioned earlier, we have to pursue friendships and romance. Such purposes are essential to a life of happiness.

Our purposes in life, according to the Objectivist ethics, are what make life *meaningful*. They are what fill our lives with intensity and subtlety and joy. They are the stuff of good living. And if our purposes are to serve their purpose, they must be chosen and pursued *rationally*. Reason and purpose go hand in hand. Having rational purposes is essential to our life and happiness.

Another value Rand identified as crucial to human life and happiness is *self-esteem*—the conviction that one is able to live and worthy of happiness. I won't say much about this, since it is a relatively obvious requirement of life and happiness. Suffice it here to say that we are not born with self-esteem; we have to *earn* it. And the only way to earn it is by thinking rationally and acting purposefully.

These three values—reason, purpose, and self-esteem—are, as Rand put it, "the three values which, together, are the means to and the realization of one's ultimate value, one's own life."[10] To live as human beings we have to think (reason); we have to choose and pursue life-promoting goals (purpose); and we have to achieve and maintain the conviction that we are able to live and worthy of happiness (self-esteem). All three are necessary for success in each area of our life.

Building on these basic values, let's turn to some key *social* principles Ayn Rand identified. We will look first at the Objectivist principle of *justice*.

"Justice," writes Rand, "is the recognition of the fact that you cannot fake the character of men as you cannot fake the character of nature. . . ."[11] Because people have free will, a person's character is what he chooses to make it. We can either recognize this fact or fail to do so—but, either way, the fact remains. A person has the character he has; he is responsible for it; and his character, whether good or bad, can affect our life accordingly. A person of *good* character can generate good ideas, create life-serving products, provide friendship or romance, become an honest politician, or in some other way have a positive impact on our life. A person of *bad* character can generate evil ideas, destroy life-serving values, deceive us, assault us, steal our property, push for life-thwarting laws, or even murder us.

Justice is the virtue of judging people rationally—according to the available and relevant *facts*—and treating them accordingly—as they *deserve* to be treated. This is the basic principle of selfish human interaction. In order to live, to protect our rights, and to achieve happiness, we have to *judge* people. "The precept: 'Judge not, that ye be not judged,'" writes Ayn Rand, "is an abdication of moral responsibility. . . . The moral principle to adopt in this issue, is: 'Judge, and be prepared to be judged.'" Quoting Rand further:

> Nothing can corrupt and disintegrate a culture or a man's character as thoroughly as does the precept of *moral agnosticism*, the idea that one must never pass moral judgment on others, that one must be morally tolerant of anything, that the good consists of never distinguishing good from evil.
>
> It is obvious who profits and who loses by such a precept. It is not justice or equal treatment that you grant to men when you abstain equally from praising men's virtues and from condemning men's vices. When your impartial attitude declares, in effect, that neither the good nor the evil may expect anything from you—whom do you betray and whom do you encourage?[12]

Only one kind of person has anything to fear from moral judgment; the rest of us can only benefit from it. Being just consists in acknowledging this fact and acting accordingly.

To live successfully, happily, and freely, we have to judge our friends, our parents, our employers and employees, our professors, and our politicians. We have to judge *everyone* who has an impact on our life. We have to judge them rationally—and treat them accordingly.

In a sense, this is so obvious that it seems silly to have to say it. But given the commonly accepted views on morality—from the biblical tenet: "Judge not that ye be not judged" to the relativist mantra: "Who are you to judge?"—not only does it have to be mentioned; it has to be stressed. *Judging people rationally and treating them accordingly is a requirement of human life.*

While those who do not care about human life might be indifferent to this fact, those of us who want to live need to take it very seriously. We need to uphold and advocate the principle of justice, and not only when it comes to condemning those who are evil, but also, and more importantly, when it comes to praising, rewarding, and defending those who are good—those who think rationally and produce the values on which human life depends: scientists who discover the laws of nature, inventors who create new life-promoting devices and medicines, businessmen who produce and market life-promoting goods and services, artists who create spiritual values that fuel our souls and bring us joy, and so on. Justice demands that we recognize such people as *good*—good *because* they self-interestedly use reason and produce life-serving values.

By studying Ayn Rand's ethics—in addition to learning a great deal more about her ideas on reason, purpose, self-esteem, and justice—you will discover the objective meaning and selfish necessity of the virtues of honesty, integrity, productiveness, and pride. In each case, Rand points to the facts that give rise to the need of such virtues; she shows why your life and happiness depend on them; and she provides an integrated philosophical system for guiding your actions accordingly.

I've merely indicated the kind of guidance offered by egoism. But in light of what we've seen so far, consider for a moment how it compares to the guidance offered by altruism. Given the many values on which human life and happiness depend—from material values, such as food, shelter, clothing, medical care, automobiles, and computers; to spiritual values, such as knowledge, self-esteem, art, friendship, and romantic love—we need a great deal of guidance in making choices and taking actions. We need moral principles that are conducive to the goal of living fully and happily over the course of years and decades. In answer to this need, egoism provides a whole system of integrated, noncontradictory principles, the sole purpose of which is to teach us how to live and enjoy life. In answer to this same need, altruism says: Don't be selfish; sacrifice your values; give up your dreams.

If we want to live and be happy, only one of these moralities will do.

And just as egoism is the only morality that provides proper guidance for our personal lives, so it is the only morality that provides a proper foundation for a civilized society. Let us turn briefly to the politics implied by egoism.

Like every ethical code, egoism has definite political implications. Just as the morality of self-sacrifice lays the groundwork for a particular kind of political system—one in which the government forces people to sacrifice (e.g., socialism, communism, fascism, theocracy)—so the morality of self-interest lays the groundwork for a certain kind of political system—one in which the government plays an entirely different role.

The basic question in politics is: What are the requirements of human life in a social context? What, in principle, must people do—or refrain from doing—in order to live together in a civilized manner? Here, Ayn Rand makes another crucial identification. Since we need to think rationally and act accordingly in order to live, we need to be *able* to act on our judgment. The only thing that can stop us from acting on our judgment is other people. And the only way they can stop us is by means of *physical force*. Quoting Rand:

> It is only by means of physical force that one man can deprive another of his life, or enslave him, or rob him, or prevent him from pursuing his own goals, or compel him to act against his own rational judgment.
>
> The precondition of a civilized society is the barring of physical force from social relationships—thus establishing the principle that if men wish to deal with one another, they may do so only by means of *reason:* by discussion, persuasion and voluntary, uncoerced agreement.[13]

If someone puts a gun to your head and tells you what to do, you cannot act on your judgment. The threat of death makes your judgment irrelevant; you now have to act on the gunman's judgment. If he says, "Give me your wallet," you have to give him your wallet. If he says, "Take off your clothes," you have to do that. If he says, "Don't object to my decrees," you must not object. You have to do whatever he says, or you'll get shot in the head. Your own judgment—your basic means of survival—has been overridden and is now useless.

And it makes no difference whether the gunman is a lone thug, or a group of thugs, or the KGB, or the senators and president of our rapidly deteriorating America. Whenever and to whatever extent physical force is used against you or me or anyone, the victim cannot act on his judgment, his basic means of living; thus, he cannot live fully as a human being. This is why rational egoism holds that the initiation of force against people is *evil.* It is evil because it is *antilife.*

On the basis of this identification, Rand established the objective case for individual rights. Since physical force used against a person is factually contrary to the requirements of his life—and since life *is* the standard of value—we need a moral principle to protect us from those who attempt to use force against us. That principle involves the concept of *rights.* Quoting Rand:

> "Rights" are a *moral* concept—the concept that provides a logical transition from the principles guiding an individual's actions to the principles guiding his relationship with others—the concept that preserves and protects individual morality in a social context—the link between the moral code of a man and the legal code of a society, between ethics and politics. *Individual rights are the means of subordinating society to moral law.* . . .
>
> A "right" is a moral principle defining and sanctioning a man's freedom of action in a social context.[14]

The key word here is *action*. Just as life is the standard of value and requires *goal-directed action*, so the *right* to life is the basic right and pertains to *freedom of action*. The right to life is the right to act as one's life requires—which means, according to one's basic means of survival—which means, on the judgment of one's own mind.

All other rights are derivatives of this fundamental right: The right to *liberty* is the right to be free from coercive interference by others. The right to *property* is the right to keep, use, and dispose of the product of one's effort. The right to the *pursuit of happiness* is the right to seek the goals and values of one's choice. The right to *freedom of speech* is the right to express one's views regardless of what others think of them.

And because a right is a sanction to action, it is *not* a sanction to be given goods or services. There can be no such thing as a "right" to be given goods or services. If a person had a "right" to be given food, or a house, or medical care, or an education, what would this imply with regard to other people? It would imply that others have to be *forced* to provide him with these goods or services. It would imply that *some* people must produce while others dispose of their product. As Rand put it: "The man who produces while others dispose of his product is a slave."

> If some men are entitled by right to the products of the work of others, it means that those others are deprived of rights and condemned to slave labor. Any alleged "right" of one man which necessitates the violation of the rights of another, is not and cannot be a right. No man can have a right to impose an unchosen obligation, an unwarranted duty or an involuntary servitude on another man. There can be no such thing as "*the right to enslave*."[15]

The North fought (and thankfully won) a legitimate war against the South on the principle that there can be no right to enslave. Rand made explicit the fundamental reason this principle is *true*. The reason each individual's life should *legally* belong to him is that each individual's life does in fact*morally* belong to him. Each individual is morally an end in himself—not a means to the ends of others. Each individual has a moral right to act on his own judgment for his own sake—and to keep, use, and dispose of the product of his effort—so long as he respects the same right of others.

The Objectivist ethics recognizes that to live as civilized beings—rather than as masters and slaves—we need a social system that protects each individual's rights to his life, liberty, property, and the pursuit of happiness. The only social system that does so—consistently and on principle—is *laissez-faire capitalism*. Quoting Rand:

> [Laissez-faire capitalism] is a system where men deal with one another, not as victims and executioners, nor as masters and slaves, but as *traders*, by free, voluntary exchange to mutual benefit. It is a system where no man may obtain any values from others by resorting to physical force, and *no man may initiate the use of physical force against others.*[16]

> The only function of the government, in such a society, is the task of protecting man's rights, *i.e.*, the task of protecting him from physical force; the government acts as the agent of man's right of self-defense, and may use force only in retaliation and only against those who initiate its use.[17]

The citizens of a laissez-faire society delegate the use of retaliatory force to the government and thus make domestic peace possible.

Of course, in an emergency situation, or when the police are not available, or when there is no time to rely on the government, citizens are morally and legally justified in using retaliatory force as necessary. (If someone comes running at you with a bowie knife, you are morally and legally justified in shooting him.) But in order to live together as civilized beings, rather than as feuding hillbillies, people must leave such force to the government whenever possible. As Rand put it, "The government is the means of placing the retaliatory use of force under *objective control*."[18]

In a capitalist society, if someone physically harms a person or damages his property or threatens to do either—and if this can be demonstrated by means of evidence—then the victim has grounds for legal recourse and, when appropriate, compensation. For instance, if someone defrauds a man, or threatens to murder him, or dumps trash in his yard, or poisons his water supply, or infringes on his patent—or in any other way causes him or his property specific harm—then the perpetrator has violated the man's rights. And if the man (or an agent on his behalf) can demonstrate that the perpetrator has done so, then he has a case against the rights violator and can seek justice in a court of law.

Properly understood, capitalism is all about enabling people to act on their own judgment, and to keep, use, and dispose of the product of their effort. It is all about stopping people from physically harming others or their property. It is all about recognizing and respecting individual rights. In other words, it is all about the requirements of human life in a social context.

Capitalism is the only social system that permits everyone to act fully according to his own judgment and thus to live fully as a human being. No other social system on earth does this. Thus, if human life is the standard of moral value, capitalism is the only moral social system.

Whereas rational egoism guides our choices and actions in pursuit of our life-serving goals and long-term happiness, laissez-faire capitalism protects individual rights by banning the initiation of physical force from social relationships. The two go hand in hand. Egoism makes human *existence* possible; capitalism makes human *coexistence* possible. Quoting Ayn Rand: "What greater virtue can one ascribe to a social system than the fact that it leaves no possibility for any man to serve his own interests by enslaving other men? What nobler system could be desired by anyone whose goal is man's well-being?"[19]

Rand has much more to say about individual rights and capitalism; I have just touched on her revolutionary principles in this regard. *Atlas Shrugged* is a hymn to capitalism and the moral foundations on which it depends. And Rand's book *Capitalism: The Unknown Ideal* is a series of essays demonstrating the vital nature of the social system, and blasting common fallacies about it. For a good understanding of the principles of capitalism, I highly recommend both books.

Reflecting on what we've discussed so far, Rand's morality of selfishness holds that, in order to live as human beings, we must pursue our life-serving values and respect the rights of others to do the same. Put negatively: We must neither sacrifice ourselves to others—nor sacrifice others to ourselves. One of the heroes in *Atlas Shrugged* put it in the form of an oath: "I swear—by my life and my love of it—that I will never live for the sake of another man, nor ask another man to live for mine." That is an oath we can all live by. But to do so, we have to repudiate the morality of sacrifice.

Rand's morality of selfishness is all about living and loving life. It is the morality of pursuing values and refusing to surrender a greater value for a lesser one. It is the morality of *non-sacrifice*. There is no reason to act in a self-sacrificial manner, which is why no one has ever given a reason to do so. Nor is there any rational justification for sacrificing others, which is why no one has ever offered one of these, either. But there *is* a reason to act in a self-interested manner: Your life and happiness depend on it.

Since we necessarily operate on a code of values of some kind while making choices in life—since morality *is* inescapable—here is the alternative that we all face in this regard: We can passively accept a morality through social osmosis—or we can think the matter through for ourselves and decide what makes sense given the observable facts. We can accept appeals to authority, tradition, popular opinion, intimidation, and the like—or we can insist on *reasons* in support of the morality we choose to accept. In other words, we can rely on the views and opinions of others—or we can rely on the judgment of our own mind.

This brings us to the final point I want to make tonight—and to what I regard as the single most important aspect of the Objectivist ethics: the principle that you should rely on your own observations and your own use of logic, the principle that you should not accept ideas just because others accept them, the principle that you should think for yourself.

Since your mind is your only means of knowledge and your basic means of achieving your goals and values, rational egoism says that—if you want to live and be happy—you must *never* surrender your mind. You must never sacrifice your judgment to anyone or anything—neither to faith, nor feelings, nor friends, nor parents, nor professors, nor Ayn Rand. And no one is more adamant about this than Rand. As she put it, "The most selfish of all things is the independent mind that recognizes no authority higher than its own and no value higher than its judgment of truth."[20]

This is the Objectivist principle of *independence*. An independent thinker relies on his *own* judgment to determine what is true or false, good or bad, right or wrong. He does not turn to others to see what he should believe or value. He may learn from others—if they are rational and have something to teach him. He may take their advice—if it makes sense to him. And he may listen to their arguments—so long as they present evidence for their claims and proceed logically. But he always makes the final judgment by means of his own thinking. In regard to any important issue, he asks himself: "What are the facts? What does the evidence say? What do *I* think?" His primary orientation is not toward other people—not toward his peers or his parents or his professors—but toward reality. And his means of assessing reality is his own use of reason.

Because rational egoism recognizes that the individual's mind is his basic means of living, it holds rational, *independent* thinking as the essence of being moral. Unlike altruism, it does not call for you to accept its principles on faith or because others say so. Rational egoism is not a dogma. It is not a set of commandments or "categorical imperatives" from on high for you to obey.

In one of Rand's essays, she tells a story of an old black woman who, in answer to a man who was telling her that she's *got to* do something or other, says, "Mister, there's nothing I've *got to* do except die."[21] Rational egoism does not say that anyone has *got to* do anything. It says only that *if* you want to live and achieve happiness—then you must observe facts, use your mind, pursue your goals, not sacrifice greater values for the sake of lesser ones, uphold the principle of individual rights, and so on. That is not dogma. It is logic. It is recognition of the law of cause and effect.

And just as Rand's ethics is not dogmatic—so it is not relativistic. It is *absolute*. It is absolute because it is based on and derived from reality—from observable facts, from the laws of nature, from the requirements of human life.

Rand exposed the false alternative of dogmatism vs. relativism. In the light of her philosophy, we are no longer faced with the ugly option of Jerry Falwell's morality vs. Jerry Springer's—or that of Bill Bennett vs. that of Bill Clinton. We now know of an *objective* ethics: one that is secular, observation-based, demonstrably true—and, best of all, *good* for you.

If you want to live a wonderful, value-laden life, you need a morality that supports that goal and guides you to act accordingly. You need a morality that upholds the value of rational, self-interested, purposeful action. Rational egoism is the only morality that does so. If you want to live in a society in which you are free to lead your life as you see fit—a society in which no one, including the government, may force you to act against your own judgment—you need a morality that is conducive to that goal. You need a morality that provides a foundation for the principle of individual rights. The only morality that does so is the Objectivist ethics.

The moral code you accept underlies and shapes everything you do in life. It determines whether you live a richly meaningful, truly happy life—or something less. And it determines whether you advocate a fully free, civilized society—or some other kind of society. I have given you just a brief sketch of Rand's ethics. There is a great deal more to it. Hopefully, I have inspired you to look further into the subject on your own.

I urge you to take a closer look at the morality that says you should live your life to the fullest and achieve the greatest happiness possible. Use your own judgment in assessing it. See if it makes sense to you. Read *Atlas Shrugged*, which is a spell-binding mystery at the heart of which is the conflict between altruism and egoism. Not only will you discover what happened to the earlier-mentioned disappearing producers; you'll also see Ayn Rand's ethics dramatized in ways that today will cause a feeling of déjà vu. Or, for a nonfiction introduction to rational egoism, read Rand's book *The Virtue of Selfishness*, which is a series of essays elaborating the groundbreaking principles of the Objectivist ethics—or my book *Loving Life: The Morality of Self-Interest and the Facts that Support It*, which is a systematic introduction to the ethics.

If you are not rationally convinced by the arguments, then do not accept them. To sacrifice your own judgment would be the most selfless thing you could do. I would never advocate such a thing—and neither would Ayn Rand. You should accept only those ideas that make sense to you.

But if you read up on this issue and *are* convinced—as I think you will be—then you can start living your life fully in accordance with the only moral code that is conducive to that goal: rational egoism—the morality Ayn Rand so appropriately called "The Morality of Life."

5

Scientific Morality and the Streetlight Effect

Night has fallen, and a police officer sees a man on his hands and knees under a streetlight looking for something. "Can I help you?" asks the officer. "Yes," says the man. "I dropped my key, and I'm having trouble finding it." The officer helps the man search for a few minutes, but to no avail. "Are you sure you dropped it here?" he asks. "Oh, no," replies the man, "I dropped it over there," pointing to a dark area across the street. "Then why are you searching for it over here?" asks the officer. "Because," says the man, "the light is over here."[1]

A similar approach can be seen among intellectuals searching for secular, objective morality.

Sam Harris, Daniel Dennett, Richard Dawkins, and other secularists claim to be searching for a rational, fact-based, scientific morality. But they are looking for it only in the "light" of socially accepted ideas. And that is not where it lies.

Today's socially accepted view of morality is that morality *equals* altruism, that being moral *means* self-sacrificially serving others—whether your neighbors, the poor, the community, or the like. And this is what Harris and company mean when they speak of morality.[2] Their goal, as Harris puts it, is to find "better reasons for self-sacrifice than those that religion provides."[3] They reject religion but embrace the notion that "being truly good" and "ethically consistent" requires "living in a way that truly maximizes the well-being of others."[4] They hold that truly moral people are those who are "inspired by their conviction that their lives [are] not their own to dispose of,"[5] those "who live their lives in effect for others."[6]

But the claim that people should self-sacrificially serve others is as *unscientific* as a claim can be. There is literally zero evidence to support it (see chapter 4).[7] This is why, throughout the entire history of philosophy, no one ever has presented such evidence.

Scientific morality—morality arising from and grounded in evidence and logic—can be found only by looking *outside* the "light" of today's socially accepted views.

To discover a fact-based, reason-based morality, one must first recognize that morality is a broader concept than altruism (see chapter 3).[8] One must see that the concept of morality subsumes several kinds or codes of morality—altruism, egoism, hedonism, utilitarianism, and others. One must acknowledge that the question of which (if any) of these codes is supported by evidence and logic is to be answered by analyzing the principles of the respective codes along with the arguments in support of them. And one must be willing to acknowledge which principles are supported by evidence and which are not.

This requires courage. It requires intellectual independence. It requires shining *the light of one's own mind* on the full scope of relevant facts and following the evidence wherever it leads.

Might it be that scientific morality is, as Ayn Rand argued, a code of observation-based principles to guide you—not in sacrificing yourself for others, nor sacrificing others for yourself—but in pursuing your life-serving values and respecting the rights of others to do the same?[9]

There's one way to find out. Turn on your light and shine it on the relevant facts.[10]

There's the key.

6

Purpose Comes from Reason, Not Religion

Purpose is one of the most important values in human life. It is the value that answers the question "What for?"—the value that motivates us to think, strive, and thrive—the value by reference to which we focus our minds, direct our actions, and pursue our goals.

And it is under assault by advocates of religion.

Religionists bastardize the concept of "purpose" (and the related concept of "meaning") in an effort to convince people—often the young—that there can be no objective purpose in life unless it comes ultimately from God.

To wit:

"If there is no God," writes theologian William Lane Craig, "there is no purpose" and "there can be no objective meaning in life."[1]

Pastor Rick Warren writes, "Without God, life has no purpose, and without purpose, life has no meaning."[2]

Dennis Prager claims, "If there is no God who designed the universe and who cares about His creations, life is ultimately purposeless," and "there is no objective meaning to life."[3]

Ben Shapiro elaborates, "God expects things of us . . . He has standards for our behavior . . . He demands our holiness"—and "His standards of truth matter, not our own." Thus, having a "moral purpose" consists in "living the life God wants for [us]"—the life God laid out for us "through a series of rules to be found in His holy book." And, Shapiro emphasizes, according to the Bible, living this way is not morally optional; it is morally mandatory: "As King Solomon concludes in Ecclesiastes, the purpose of human existence is simple: *"Fear God and keep his commandments, for this is the whole duty of man."*[4]

Why is this our duty? Why must we obey God's commandments and live the life he wants for us? Pastor Warren answers: "You exist only because God wills that you exist. You were made *by* God and *for* God. . . . It is only in God that we discover our origin, our identity, our meaning, our purpose, our significance, and our destiny."[5]

What about personal fulfillment? What if you want to live in accordance with *your own* judgment and embrace purposes of *your own* choosing—purposes such as a career that you love and that challenges you and rewards your efforts; recreational activities and friendships that fuel your soul; a romantic relationship full of love, laughter, and pleasure; dreams and ambitions that motivate you constantly to strive, improve, and enjoy life all the more? In other words, what if you want the purpose of your life to be the achievement of your own happiness? After all, it is *your* life. Shouldn't the purpose of your life be about *you*?

Not according to religion. As pastor Warren writes:

> It's not about you. The purpose of your life is far greater than your own personal fulfillment, your peace of mind, or even your happiness. It's far greater than your family, your career, or even your wildest dreams and ambitions.

> If you want to know why you were placed on this planet, you must begin with God. You were born *by* his purpose and *for* his purpose.[6]

What does it mean to live for God's purpose? How exactly does one do this? Pastor Warren explains:

> To fulfill your mission will require that you abandon your agenda and accept God's agenda for your life. . . . You must say, like Jesus, "*Father, . . . I want your will, not mine.*" You yield your rights, expectations, dreams, plans, and ambitions to him. You stop praying selfish prayers like "God bless what I want to do." Instead you pray, "God help me to do what you're blessing!" You hand God a blank sheet with your name signed at the bottom and tell him to fill in the details. The Bible says, "*Give yourselves completely to God—every part of you . . . to be tools in the hands of God, to be used for his good purposes.*"[7]

Such is the nature of purpose according to religion: God exists, he created you, he has standards for your behavior, and he has a purpose for your life. Thus, you have a "duty" to abandon your agenda, obey his commands, be a tool for his purposes, and live the life he wants for you. "This is the whole duty of man."

But this is *not* the "duty" of man. This is *not* the nature of purpose. And it is crucial to understand what is wrong with these ideas, to reject them, and to expose them as the dangerous nonsense that they are.

A purpose is the reason or intention for which an action is taken or a thing is created or used. For instance, my purpose in writing this article is to clarify the secular source and vital importance of purpose. The purpose of a sermon is to convey the word of "God." The purpose of a car is to transport people or goods. The purpose of friendship is to enjoy each other's company and the fruits of mutual interests, respect, and affection.

One of the most important purposes in a person's life is his career or the work he does. And the meaning of a person's work can be profound. Consider, for example, the career goals and achievements of a few figures of note.

Andrew Carnegie sought to improve the ways in which businesses and business activities are integrated so as to make them extremely efficient, productive, and profitable. When he turned his focus and aim to the steel industry, he created one of the most profitable and life-serving businesses in history. Carnegie Steel Company fueled industrialization and the construction of modern America, and Carnegie's management techniques and inventions changed the way businesses are integrated and operated to this day.[8]

Louis Pasteur is most widely known for his invention of pasteurization, which is crucial to the preservation and safety of dairy products and other foods. But Pasteur did much more than that. He also made several important discoveries in chemistry, launched the fields of microbiology and immunology, cured multiple diseases, and developed the first vaccines for rabies and anthrax.[9]

Katharine Hepburn was a leading lady in Hollywood for more than six decades, starring in movies such as *Little Women* (1933), *Bringing Up Baby* (1938), *The African Queen* (1951), *Guess Who's Coming to Dinner* (1967), and *On Golden Pond* (1981). In addition to delighting and moving audiences by doing work she loved and doing it her way, she received a record four Academy Awards for Best Actress and was named by the American Film Institute "the greatest female star of Classic Hollywood Cinema."[10]

Ayn Rand wrote some of the most profound and philosophically rich novels of all time, including *The Fountainhead* and *Atlas Shrugged*. She also created the philosophy of Objectivism, "a philosophy for living on earth." In the course of creating it, she solved several perennial and pressing problems in the history of philosophy, including "the problem of universals" (how concepts are formed and what they refer to) and the "is–ought problem" (how moral principles, including individual rights, are derived from perceptual reality).

Each of these individuals was extremely purpose driven. Each lived a rich, productive, fulfilling life. And each left the world a better place.

Did *they* hand God a blank sheet with their names signed at the bottom and tell him to fill in the details? Hardly. All of them were atheists—as were and are countless other purposeful and productive people. Other well-known atheists include Thomas Edison, Frank Lloyd Wright, Bruce Lee, Richard Branson, John Cleese, Ricky Gervais, Julia Sweeney, Albert Ellis, Jonathan Haidt, Abraham Maslow, Emma Thompson, Thandie Newton, Oscar Wilde, Mark Zuckerberg, Tim Minchin, Ayaan Hirsi Ali, Clarence Darrow, Keira Knightley, Richard Feynman, and many more.

Of course, not all atheists are rational, rights-respecting people. And not everyone with aims embraces rational, rights-respecting purposes. Some people—including some atheists and religionists—pursue irrational, rights-violating, even massively destructive aims. Mao Tse-tung sought to impose communism on the people of China and murdered upwards of seventy million people in the process. Adolf Hitler sought to impose national socialism on the people of Germany (and ultimately the world) and to prop up so-called Aryans as the "master race"; in the process, he orchestrated the murder of approximately six million Jewish people and eleven million people of other races. Hugo Chávez and Nicolás Maduro sought to impose socialism on the people of Venezuela and drove them into poverty, mass suffering, and early graves (this continues today, so the total destruction is not yet known). Osama bin Laden sought to impose Islam on the world and orchestrated the murder, rape, and submission of countless men, women, and children in the name of Allah. With that same aim, Khalid Sheikh Mohammed and the 9/11 hijackers sought to murder as many "infidel" Americans as possible by flying passenger jets into government buildings and skyscrapers full of people.

Did these monsters have "purposes"? In a sense, they did. They had *evil* purposes.

What distinguishes moral purposes from evil ones? This question goes to the crux of the matter at hand.

The fundamental difference between a moral purpose and an immoral purpose is that the former is based on, or consonant with, the principle that the requirements of human life and happiness constitute the standard of moral value; the latter is not. Because human beings are *individuals*, this standard pertains to individuals—including *all* individuals. It means that the good is that which advances an individual's life and happiness without violating the rights of other individuals to their lives or the pursuit of their happiness (so, without murdering them, assaulting them, or physically forcing them to act against their own judgment). Consequently, this standard is incompatible with standards such as "the good of the community," "the good of society," "the good of the race," or "the will of God"—all of which place something over and above the life and the rights of the individual.

The principle that in order for human values or moral evaluations to be correct, they must be consonant with the factual requirements of human life and happiness was discovered and elucidated by Ayn Rand.[11] This principle is derived from observation and logic; thus, it is demonstrably true.[12] (Look and see.)

And because it *is* true, it is the objective standard by reference to which we can judge a given purpose as moral or immoral.

God's will logically cannot dictate a proper purpose because God does not exist—which is why (a) there is no evidence for his existence, and (b) no one has ever provided such evidence. That for which there is no evidence cannot rationally be said to exist, much less to dictate a proper purpose or to be an objective standard of morality.

And given the many atrocities and rights violations that God commits and commands in religious scripture, it's a good thing he doesn't exist. For example, in the Bible, God deliberately drowns practically everyone on earth[13] and calls for the murder of blasphemers,[14] infidels,[15] homosexuals,[16]and children who curse or disobey their parents.[17] He also condones slavery[18] and rape.[19] Likewise, in the Koran, God calls for the murder of unbelievers [20] and for making sex slaves of their wives and daughters.[21]

Religionists advise you to "hand [*that*] God a blank sheet with your name signed at the bottom and tell him to fill in the details"?! Imagine the monster you might become if you did.

Neither God nor religion is (or can be) the source of moral purpose in your life. The source of such purpose is your reasoning mind.

Whereas there is no evidence for the existence of God, there is a *world* of evidence supporting the principle that, if we want to live and flourish, we must choose and pursue purposes *rationally*: We must look at reality; discover the requirements of our life and happiness; choose our preferences and purposes from within the vast range of rational, life-serving, rights-respecting options; and pursue them with everything we have. This is the way—and the only way—to choose and pursue morally correct purposes.

"But," religionists will argue, "your rational, secular approach to purpose doesn't answer the question 'What is the purpose of life?'"[22] About this they will be right. (But they won't like the reason.)

The question, "What is the purpose of life?" is logically invalid. It's a classic case of the fallacy of the loaded question. As Ayn Rand observed:

> It smuggles in a wrong answer. The question should be: "What is the purpose of *your* life?"—"What is the purpose of *my* life?"—"What is the purpose of each particular individual about whom we inquire?" But not: "What is the purpose of life?" Asked that way, it seems to imply that somebody outside of us—naturally some "supernatural" being—is the one who has to prescribe that purpose, and we should spend our life trying to find it out and then live up to it. There is no such thing as "the purpose of life" [in that sense], because life is an end in itself.
>
> *Life* is the purpose of life. . . . You should *enjoy* your life. You should *be happy* in it. Your proper, moral obligation is to pursue the highest form of happiness possible to you. . . . Any person who attempts to prescribe—not even enforce, *just prescribe*—the happiness of other people is a monster and has no claim to morality at all.[23]

You live once. Then you die, and your life is over forever. Your life—including all of the values, experiences, efforts, achievements, and relationships that make up your life—properly matters more to you than anything else in the world. The moral question to ask yourself is not "How can I be a tool in the hands of God?"—but "How can I make my life the best, happiest life it can be?"

Moral purpose is life-serving, rights-respecting purpose. And your means of identifying, choosing, and pursuing such purpose is your reasoning mind.

Use it and thrive.

7

Purpose, Value Hierarchies, and Happiness

That we live only once is not speculation. This is it. This life is all we have. This fact, however, is not cause for despair; it is cause for action.

To quote a favorite ad, "It's not that life's too short, it's just that you're dead for so long." Our time in life is substantial—we might live to eighty, ninety, or even a hundred years old—and we can do a great deal in the decades we have. But we are going to die. And when we do, that's it. We're done. So: What to do?

As rational egoists—as people who know that the moral purpose of life is to maximize our personal happiness—we want to fill our days and years with accomplishments and joy. We want to wake up every morning and pursue our values with vigor. We want to thrive in a career we love, in romance, in our recreational pursuits, in our friendships, and so on. In short, we want to make our lives the best they can be.

Author's note: This essay is an edited version of a lecture I've delivered to various Objectivist community groups. It assumes some understanding of and agreement with the philosophy of Objectivism.

That's easy to say. And, in a sense, it's easy to do: Just think rationally and act accordingly. In another sense, however, it is the single most difficult thing in the world.

Making our life the best it can be is the only project that requires the harmonious use of *all* of our resources and capacities—physical and mental, personal and social—toward a highly complex goal for the span of our entire life. No other project comes even close to this in terms of its demands. In fact, all of our other egoistic endeavors are subsumed under this one. Whether we are performing brain surgery, or composing a symphony, or building a semiconductor company, or raising children, or learning to hang glide—all such endeavors are only projects *within* the broader goal of making the most of our life. Everything we do is but an aspect of this grand, all-encompassing goal.

To achieve the greatest happiness possible, we have to unify all of our choices, values, and goals into a single harmonious whole. This requires a great deal of thinking, selecting, planning, prioritizing, coordinating, reviewing, reevaluating, and so on. At every turn, we must gain or apply the necessary knowledge, use our best judgment, and act accordingly—with respect to the full context of our values and goals.

This is a huge subject, and, in keeping with the opening point, we have limited time. So I want to be clear about the scope of my talk. My goal tonight is to indicate the nature and importance of purpose (and related matters) in good living. My overarching point is that understanding and upholding the concept, value, and principle of purpose is essential to making your life the best it can be.

What is a purpose? It's a kind of goal—specifically, a conscious, intentional goal, a goal chosen and pursued for a desired outcome. Not all goals are purposes. For example, although plants have goals, in that they act to gain or keep things (e.g., sunlight and water), plants are not conscious and thus cannot engage in intentional action. Only certain conscious animals can act purposefully. Nor are all purposes equal in significance or scope. Although dolphins are conscious and may act intentionally or purposefully in a certain respect (e.g., they try to catch fish and may even help people or other animals in trouble in water), such intentions or purposes are orders of magnitude different from the kinds of long-range, wide-range, conceptual goals that human beings choose and pursue—such as, "I'm going to create an institute for the study of the cognitive capacities of sea life." A purpose in the sense that we are talking about here is a volitional and *conceptual* goal.

Although the concept of purpose is narrower than that of goal (in that all purposes are goals but not vice versa), purpose is nevertheless a very broad concept—broader than some egoists or Objectivists might think. And grasping its breadth is essential to employing this cardinal value toward maximizing our personal happiness.

Importantly, purpose is not the equivalent of central purpose. A central purpose is a *kind* of purpose, namely, a primary long-range productive goal, the central goal around which one integrates all of one's other projects and goals.[1] Depending on one's age and circumstances, one's central purpose might be completing school, building a business, advancing one's career, raising one's children—or working toward selecting a central purpose. But such goals do not exhaust the meaning of purpose. Purpose is much broader and much deeper than that, and, if we want to think clearly about how to live selfishly, we need to understand and employ the concept and value of purpose in all its breadth and depth.

To treat central purpose as the equivalent of purpose is to commit the fallacy of the frozen abstraction. It is to freeze the concept of purpose at the level of one of the narrower abstractions that is subsumed under it, and thus to omit from the broader concept all of the other crucially important kinds of purposes—purposes we need to conceptualize, embrace, and pursue if we are to live fully. Among the many purposes that are omitted from the concept of purpose by the commission of this fallacy is the moral purpose of life, which is the achievement of your personal happiness. That is not something you want to omit from your thinking!

Life is not all about work—it is all about achieving happiness. If we want to achieve the greatest happiness possible, we must pursue many purposes in addition to our central purpose. We must pursue romantic relationships, recreational activities, leisure activities, friendships, homes, vacations, adventures, and so on. These are not central purposes, but they are crucial, life-serving purposes. And if we want to make the most of our lives, we must see them as such, conceptualize them as such, and proceed to design our lives accordingly.

Religionists are right about two things: There is a designer, and he is intelligent. But he is not God. He is *you*. And what he designs is not the universe, but *your* universe: your life.

Living fully purposefully consists in intelligently designing every aspect of your life that is open to your choice. This means always acting with a specific life-serving purpose in mind—whether in regard to work, play, romance, or rest. Put negatively, it means never acting aimlessly.

Here's a relevant passage you may recall from *Atlas Shrugged*:

> "I don't know what sort of motto the d'Anconias have on their family crest," Mrs. Taggart said once, "but I'm sure that Francisco will change it to 'What for?'" It was the first question he asked about any activity proposed to him—and nothing would make him act, if he found no

> valid answer. He flew through the days of his summer months like a rocket, but if one stopped him in midflight, he could always name the purpose of his every random moment. Two things were impossible to him: to stand still or to move aimlessly.[2]

"What for?" means "For what *purpose*?"

The question "What's the purpose?" regarding any given endeavor is the question: "What does this mean for my life?"

Purpose, like reason, is *fundamental* in the Objectivist ethics because it is fundamental to good living. In a certain respect, purpose is even more fundamental than reason.

Reason is our basic value—but only because it is our basic means of achieving our basic *purpose*: that of living and loving life. This purpose necessitates reason, not vice versa. This purpose makes reason a value, not vice versa. This purpose is the end; reason is the means.

This means-end relationship holds not only with respect to our most basic purpose, but with respect to *all* of our purposes. We need to use reason if we want to succeed in our career—if we want to enjoy our recreational activities—if we want to establish and maintain good relationships—if we want to defend our rights—and so on.

Reason is, as Rand put it, "a purposefully directed process of cognition."[3] We think in order to gain knowledge of the world and our needs—so that we can act accordingly—so that we can achieve our chosen goals—so that we can live and love life. Reason is a value because it serves our purposes—and *only* because it serves them. To put it most starkly: Apart from our purposes, reason wouldn't even be a value.

This fact in no way diminishes the value of reason. Reason, not purpose, is our means of knowledge. Reason, not purpose, is our basic means of survival. The only way to identify the requirements of life and happiness is by using reason.

The only way to choose or pursue valid, life-serving purposes is by means of reason. Reason is our supreme life-serving value.

So the point of my emphasis here is not to demote reason, but to *promote* purpose—or, more accurately, to recognize it for what it really is.

Recognizing the full breadth and depth of the concept and value of purpose is essential to understanding and embracing a closely related and crucial tool—the *principle* of purpose: the fundamental truth that, if you want to make your life the best it can be, you must be consciously goal-directed in every aspect of your life where choice applies.[4]

To say that this is a demanding principle would be quite an understatement, so, before we consider how to uphold it, let's be emphatically clear about the answer to "What for?".

What is the purpose of this principle? Well, it's not to uphold the categorical imperative that "thou shalt be purposeful!" There is no such thing as a categorical imperative. There are only conditional imperatives, such as: If you want to maximize your happiness in life, then you must embrace the means to that end. The purpose of being fully purposeful is to achieve the greatest happiness possible.

At any time, in regard to any endeavor, without conscious reference to a rational, life-serving purpose, you cannot know what is good for your life or bad for it, whether in regard to crucially important matters or in regard to relatively trivial ones. Consider, for instance, cleaning your house. How clean is clean enough? Should you sterilize the place? Without a purpose in mind, you could waste a lot of time scrubbing tiles.

Consider exercising or working out. How much is enough? Should you make yourself as fit as an Olympian? You wouldn't get much else done if you did. The question is: Fit for what? What is your purpose here? Are you aiming to win some major athletic competition, or are you just trying to stay healthy, energetic, and attractive? Your proper level of fitness depends on your purposes in life—and you can't decide on that proper level without reference to those purposes.

Take studying philosophy. Which philosophers should you study? Which branches should you focus on? Which problems or questions should you tackle? How much time—if any—should you spend on this? Assuming you're not a professional philosopher, if you spent as much time studying philosophy as professional philosophers do, your other values—such as your career, your business, your love life, and your health—would suffer severely. And if you are going to study this vast subject profitably, you need to know what you are trying to get from it so you can guide your studies accordingly.

How about the vital activity of introspecting? How much time should you spend on this? A few minutes per month? A few hours per week? Days on end? It depends on what you are trying to accomplish. Is your goal to routinely monitor your mental processes, ideas, and emotions so that you can think clearly and act accordingly? Or are you working with a therapist to unearth some deep-rooted psychological problem that is wrecking your life? Or are you doing research for a book you're writing on the process and value of introspecting? Your purpose makes a difference.

If a person thinks or acts without respect to consciously chosen, life-serving goals, then he is proceeding either "from duty" (like a Kantian robot) or aimlessly (like a Kerouacian hippie). Either way, he is not being selfish—and he will pay the price. He will find himself either strapped by bogus obligations—or awash in a sea of concretes without the abstractions necessary to navigate life.

Your purposes not only guide you; they *are* you. There is no *self* apart from one's purposes; there is no you apart from your chosen goals. What you choose to do and how you choose to do it *is* who you are.

If you want to make the most of your life, then, no matter what you are doing at any given time, you should know *why* you are doing it. You should know the purpose of the activity in relation to the full context of your values and goals. Whether you are designing an oil rig, or watching a movie, or receiving a massage, or running a marathon, you should know *why*—given the full context of your knowledge and values—this is what you should be doing right now. There is no "duty" to know why; there is only the fact that you live only once and that every precious, irretrievable moment of your life is spent either in optimal service of your life and happiness or in some suboptimal way.

Consider what this means in regard to the major areas of life.

The major areas of life include career, romance, recreation, friendship, and, if you have children, parenting. There are essentially two ways to approach each of these areas: fully purposefully or less than fully purposefully. What does it mean to be fully purposeful in one of these areas? It means to rationally determine exactly what you want—and then to selfishly pursue it to the best of your ability.

Take central purpose first. Have you chosen your career or education goals by reference to the full context of your values and options? Have you done due diligence here? Or have you fallen into your job (or, if in college, your major) because it was convenient or expected of you? Are you pursuing your central purpose with passion and rigor; are you thinking through every aspect of this crucial mission and putting forth your best effort at every turn? Or are you occasionally coasting in regard to this vital and defining issue? (Coasting here doesn't mean doing other important, life-serving things in addition to your central purpose; rather, it means pursuing your central purpose in a less than fully selfish way.) Your central purpose is the main source of your self-esteem and happiness in life. Coasting is not a selfish option.

Take romance. Do you really know what you want in a romantic relationship—and are you making a concerted effort to achieve or maintain it? Or are you loafing on the love front? If you're single, have you thought out the essential qualities you want in a romantic partner? Or are you relying on unexamined emotional reactions to potential candidates? Are you actively pursuing romance? Or are you waiting for it to knock on your door? If you have a lover, are you treating him or her as the crucial value he or she is to you? Do you express your love openly and justly? Do you work rationally to keep the relationship alive, fresh, exciting, rewarding? Or are you coasting in an emotional auto-mode of some sort?

Our emotions are crucially important—especially in the realm of romance—but they cannot tell us who is good or bad for our life, or how to establish or maintain wonderful, life-enhancing relationships. Only reason can—and *only* if we choose to apply it with respect to our life-serving purposes.

Take recreation. Have you chosen your recreational activities purposefully? Have you considered the relevant alternatives and zeroed in on the ones that are likely to bring you the greatest joy? Or have you just fallen into something by accident or mere convenience? Playing basketball might be a perfect recreational activity for you—or it might not. It depends on whether you've made the determination on the basis of selfish due diligence. If you just happen to play basketball because there's a court near your house, then you might be (and probably are) missing out on an alternative that you would find more rewarding—perhaps kayaking or ballroom dancing or horseback riding—which you would discover if you were to approach the issue fully purposefully.

Take friendship. Who are your friends? With whom do you spend your precious social time? Who do you dine with, ski with, chat with over a beer? There are a whole lot of people out there. Do you engage with interesting, virtuous ones—people who deserve your company and bring you great joy? Or do you spend your time and energy in mediocre relationships—or worse? Meeting interesting and good people is not always easy, but hanging out with uninteresting or unethical folks is no way to make an effort. You can always visit a new coffeehouse, join a different gym, try a new hobby, or the like and meet new people in the process. If you want wonderful, life-enhancing relationships, you must make a conscious, purposeful effort.

If you are a parent, similar questions apply. Are you doing your best to provide your child with rational guidance, good education, and opportunities to explore his interests? Do you have a rational, purposeful approach to parenting? Or are you just winging it? The rewards of parenting are largely a result of the rationality and purposefulness of one's parenting program.

Living purposefully means being thoughtful about *everything* you do. It means being fully intentional at every turn. It means living your life like it's your only one—which, of course, it is.

It is a simple but profound truth that our time is limited and that every moment that passes is really gone forever. This fact gives rise to what I call *the principle of non-neutrality*. There is no such thing as a neutral action. Since the hours and days of life are limited and irretrievable, to spend any time doing something that is not good for your life is to act in a manner that is bad for your life. Any action that does not promote your life thereby squanders it.

This means that not only is drifting not pro-life; it is *anti-*life—and any degree of it is anti-life. To the extent that we are not acting consciously on behalf of chosen life-serving values, we are acting self*less*ly. And if we do not establish our purposes, organize them rationally, and pursue them accordingly, then we *will* drift; we will live less than fully purposefully—which means less than fully selfishly—which means less than fully happily.

Now, this doesn't mean that we should panic if we find ourselves drifting. That would serve no purpose! Rather, it means that we should commit (or recommit) ourselves to living fully purposefully.

Living purposefully means seeing every moment of every day as a precious, irreplaceable part of an integrated whole—and acting accordingly.

What practical steps are necessary to live this way? One crucial step is to explicitly organize and prioritize our values and goals with respect to their relative importance to our life and happiness.

Consider a highly relevant passage from Rand's *Introduction to Objectivist Epistemology*. Bear in mind here that "telos" means "end" or "goal"; thus "teleological" means "goal-directed." A teleological measurement is a value calculation made with respect to the relative importance of a number of goals or values.

> A moral code is a set of abstract principles; to practice it, an individual must translate it into the appropriate concretes—he must choose the particular goals and values which he is to pursue. This requires that he define his particular hierarchy of values, in the order of their importance, and that he act accordingly. Thus all his actions have to be guided by a process of teleological measurement. (The degree of uncertainty and contradictions in a man's hierarchy of values is the degree to which he will be unable to perform such measurements and will fail in his attempts at value calculations or at purposeful action.)

> Teleological measurement has to be performed in and against an enormous context: it consists of establishing the relationship of a given choice to all the other possible choices and to one's hierarchy of values.
>
> The simplest example of this process, which all men practice (with various degrees of precision and success), may be seen in the realm of material values—in the (implicit) principles that guide a man's spending of money. On any level of income, a man's money is a limited quantity; in spending it, he weighs the value of his purchase against the value of every other purchase open to him for the same amount of money, he weighs it against the hierarchy of all his other goals, desires and needs, then makes the purchase or not accordingly.
>
> The same kind of measurement guides man's actions in the wider realm of moral or spiritual values. (By "spiritual" I mean "pertaining to consciousness." I say "wider" because it is man's hierarchy of values in this realm that determines his hierarchy of values in the material or economic realm.) But the currency or medium of exchange is different. In the spiritual realm, the currency—which exists in limited quantity and must be teleologically measured in the pursuit of any value—is *time*, i.e., *one's life*.[5]

The crucial points here for our present purpose are: (1) Our fundamental currency in life—the thing we spend one way or another depending on the clarity and consistency of our value hierarchy (or lack thereof)—is our *time*, which *is* our life. They're the same thing. (2) If we don't have our values organized and prioritized with respect to their relative importance—and thus integrated into a noncontradictory life-serving whole—we can't even *think* in a consistently selfish manner, let alone act in a consistently selfish manner.

The first point is relatively obvious: Our time is our life. What we do with our time—and how we do it—is what we make of our life. The second point, although not immediately obvious, is on examination true. "Should I go to the ball game this Saturday? Or should I go to the office and work?" Observe that the question cannot be rationally answered without knowing how these alternatives fit into the hierarchy and network of my other values, needs, goals, purposes. What is the nature of this ball game? Is my son or daughter playing in it? What is my situation at work? Is this Monday the deadline for a major project? What is the context here? What other values and aspects of my life are relevant to my making this decision? And, given that context, what matters most?

To think rationally—to think selfishly—we must organize our values hierarchically and refer to them regularly. Some of the elements of the hierarchy are relatively straightforward. Our career (or our need to choose one) is certainly going to be one of our top values, as are our health, our romantic interests, and, if we have children, our children. And each of these top values entails or implies many related values, elements, and aspects. Plus there are all of our other values—recreation, friendships, art, fitness, home improvements, travel, and so on—along with all of the aspects of these values and goals. If we want to think clearly about our choices, goals, and actions in life, we need to know how our values relate to one another. We need a value hierarchy that includes and accounts for the many things that matter to our happiness.

If I want to lose my gut or strengthen my quads or the like but don't include this goal in my value hierarchy in a way that integrates with my other values, then I will not put sufficient mental attention toward this goal to generate the kind of physical effort required to achieve it. Likewise, if I want to travel but don't include travel goals in my value hierarchy in a way that integrates with my other values, then I won't be able to think clearly about travel or related matters; thus, among other problems, I may only fantasize about travel, rather than actually do it.

To make objective calculations and decisions about what is best for our life and happiness, we must establish and maintain a personal and rational value hierarchy; and we must refer to it regularly, review it periodically, and revise it as necessary over the course of our life. I discuss this process and related matters in detail in my forthcoming book, *Thinking in Principles: The Science of Selfishness*, but I'll touch on a few essentials here.

The first thing to note is that mere desires are not the same thing as values. Values are not just things we dream about or long for; rather, they are things we *act* to gain or keep. The key word here is: act. If we dream about someday starting our own business but never take action toward making that a reality, then we don't truly value it. Values are objects of actions.

The second and related thing to note is that we have a value hierarchy of some sort already, whether or not we're conscious of it. Our existing value hierarchy consists of whatever we recently have been and currently are acting to gain or keep. This may or may not be the value hierarchy we want; it may not be consistent with our genuinely self-interested needs and desires. But if we have been taking action at all—which, of course, we have—then we've been allotting time to the corresponding goals and thereby assigning them relative value. Toward establishing and pursuing the hierarchy we *want*, the starting point is to identify the one we have and then compare it to the one we want so that we can see the changes we need to make.

To identify your actual value hierarchy, look back at the past few months of your life, observe how you have actually spent your time, and write down all the major time expenditures on paper or on your preferred electronic device. (Omit normal, healthy sleep hours, but include extra sleep necessitated by heavy drinking or the like.) Writing down these items is crucial because there will be too many units to retain otherwise, and because you'll need to be able to see the big picture and all of its parts in order to make selfish use of the hierarchy.

What have you been doing with your time? If you've been working fifty hours per week at a job you love, then you've been valuing that job that much. If you've been working fifty hours per week at a job you loathe, you've been valuing *that* job that much. If you've been watching television for two hours per night, then you've been valuing the shows you've been watching—and valuing them above all other possible uses of that time. If you've been taking ballroom dancing lessons for a few hours per week, then you've been valuing those lessons above all other possible uses of that time. If you've been engaging with your lover in the evenings, then you've been valuing him or her accordingly. If you've been building an addition onto your house during the weekends, or going sailing on Sunday afternoons, or taking aikido lessons on Thursday evenings, or hanging out with friends on Friday nights, or sleeping all day on Saturdays—then you've been valuing that particular engagement to that extent. And so on.

Once you have accounted for all of the major time expenditures in your recent past, simply arrange the items with respect to the amount of time you've spent on each, and there, roughly, is your hierarchy of values. (There is also the matter of the *quality* of the effort exerted in these areas, but I'm setting this aside here, as our time is limited.) This value hierarchy may or may not portray the life you want to be living. But it provides an enormous value toward making change, if that is what you want to do.

(It is important to note here that although we may spend the majority of our waking hours working, one of the reasons we do this is that our work enables us to pursue all of our other values.

Our work provides us with money for food, homes, and countless other material values; it provides us with self-confidence and self-respect, which improve all aspects of our life; and it buys us time to spend on recreation, leisure, and—most importantly—with the people we love. So bear in mind that the fact that we spend more time working than we do with our loved ones does not mean that we value work more than we value them; rather, it means that we recognize, implicitly if not explicitly, the integrated nature of our values and the causal relationships involved.)

With your actual value hierarchy in hand, you can fruitfully turn to your *desired* hierarchy. Here the overarching question is: What do you *want* to do with your time?, which means: What do you *want* to make of your life? The goal is to write down what you want in each major or significant area of your life, and to begin arranging these potential goals in an integrated, noncontradictory way—prioritizing the things you want most, subordinating the things that matter less, and eliminating or postponing the things that can't be integrated at this time. (If you want to move to Denver *and* go surfing every day, something has to give.)

Your life is yours to design, and you can design it intelligently or otherwise. As an egoist, you want to design it intelligently. And your only limitation is the law of causality. You know the proverb that Rand said captures the essence of the Objectivist ethics—"God said: 'Take what you want, and pay for it'"—that's what this is all about. What do you want? And what must you do to get it?

The goal here is to put down on paper a blueprint of your ideal life—*all* the things you want to do during this one, limited, precious life you have—so that you can begin taking specific actions to design your life in the image of your selfish desires. Once you have both your actual and your desired value hierarchies in front of your eyes, you can begin to identify the changes you need to enact (if any) toward making your life the best it can be.

(For more on value hierarchies and related matters, including principles and techniques for breaking down complex goals into subgoals and ultimately into specific action steps, see *Thinking in Principles*.)

Of course, in addition to organizing and hierarchizing our desired values, we have to commit ourselves to doing our very best in pursuing and enjoying them. Given our time restraints, I can't say much on this subject tonight, but I want to touch briefly on the essence of the matter and mention a few helpful principles and standing orders.

The essence of the issue here is that we have to commit ourselves to the virtue of *pride*—the virtue of upholding all of the virtues all of the time—the virtue of moral ambitiousness.[6] Contrary to the tenets of fantasy philosophies (such as religion and Kantianism), moral perfection is not only possible, it is also necessary if you want to make your life the best it can be. Moral perfection does not mean never making an innocent mistake or an error of knowledge. Rather it means always using your best judgment given your knowledge. If your values are in selfish order, and if you keep them that way by adjusting your value hierarchy in accordance with your rational desires as a matter of course, then you *can* act in a consistently selfish manner—and thereby (literally) make your life the best it can be.

I assume that you are familiar with the major Objectivist virtues—rationality, honesty, integrity, and the like—so I'm not going to say much about them here. But I do want to point out the necessity and beauty of converting these highly abstract principles into more specific guides to thought and action—guides that take into account *your* personal needs, *your* personal context, *your* personal strengths and weaknesses, *your* particular purposes.

The precepts to always go by reason, never fake reality, always uphold rational principles, be morally ambitious, and the like are so abstract that if we don't convert them into more specific principles of action, we are not likely to succeed in our efforts at upholding them. We need personal techniques, standing orders, and principles of action that work for us, given our specific circumstances.

I have developed several that I find very helpful, and I'll present a few here just to indicate what I have in mind and how they work.

One standing order I use is "Go about your business." I'm sure you are familiar with various "business and life" analogies, but this one—in conjunction with the Objectivist ethics—is particularly profound. Just as the saying "Time is life" is cliché but true, so too for "Life is business."

Living consists in producing, consuming, and trading values—both material and spiritual. We produce goods and services, whether cattle or automobiles or medical care or the like; and we produce spiritual values, such as ideas, moral character, and self-esteem. All of this is currency in the business of life. As egoists, we are constantly producing and trading. We live by "doing business."

Take "your business" here to mean your well-thought-out hierarchy of values, the full context of your circumstances, and the causes necessary to achieve your goals. This standing order—"Go about your business"—helps you to remain selfish when your immediate desires or emotions might distract you from the actual, considered hierarchy of your values and your plans to achieve them. For instance, suppose there is a party tonight that you would love to attend, but you have a crucial deadline tomorrow—such as a term paper or a business proposal—and you must work tonight to make it. Depending on the state of your subconscious, the thought of the party might be distracting—even seductive. It could even make you feel as though going to the party would really be in your best interest. The standing order "Go about your business" reminds you that you've already established what is in your best interest; you already have a plan. It reminds you that you've already thought this through, already established what matters most, already made the selfish decision. Thus, it frees you of the shortsighted temptation to commit what would in this context be a sacrifice.

"Go about your business" can also be helpful when the next task you need to do in some endeavor is unpleasant or infuriating—say, cleaning out your chaotic closet or having to attend a "diversity" training class where you work. Likewise, it can be helpful when the going gets tough—say, you lose a major customer or get fired or break up with your lover. Such losses can *feel* like the end of the world, but if you remind yourself of the full context of your values—of the master plan of which these are aspects—then you can refocus your energy on the positive and move forward.

As an egoist, "your business" is to be true to the full context of your selfish values by respecting their hierarchy and enacting the causes necessary to achieve them. Do you ever find yourself procrastinating? "Go about your business!" Watching too much television? "Go about your business!" Avoiding the gym? Dwelling on losses or misfortunes of the past? Spending too much time on Facebook? "Go about your business!"

Just as angel investors are looking for return on investment, so too are we ego investors. Our investment in life is our time and effort. The return we are seeking is a life filled with values and happiness. Where we choose to put our time and effort largely determines our success or failure.

Decide what you want, organize your values accordingly, and "Go about your business."

Another business-oriented standing order I use is "Focus on the benefits." This one helps with motivation—specifically, motivation by values or love as against motivation by pain or fear, the carrot as against the stick.

Why do advertising and marketing specialists recommend to businessmen that they "sell the benefits, not the features" of their products? The reason is that the general (and correct) assumption of the marketplace is that people are largely motivated by their selfish values, that they want to know "What's in it for me?". As Objectivists, we recognize the deeper truth that the only legitimate reason why we (or anyone) should do anything is because we can see what is in it for us. As Francisco insists, "What for?"

Do you need to wake up at 4 A.M. in order to work on that business plan before going to work so you can start your own company this year? Getting out of bed that early can be difficult. But if, when the alarm goes off, you immediately enact the standing order to "Focus on the benefits" of getting this thing done, you can draw yourself out of bed with relative ease. The trick is to picture the benefits as vividly as possible: that beautiful restaurant with the bougainvillea-covered pergola, your happy customers sitting at linen-topped tables ordering your best bottles of wine to go with your melt-in-the-mouth duck breast, the glowing reviews on Yelp and Urban Spoon, the financial security for you and your family . . . The aim is to focus not on the feature—in this case, the writing of the business plan—but on the reason you are writing it: the "What for?". Once you are out of bed and have had some coffee, you can turn your attention to the feature, at which time you'll find yourself pleasantly eager to write it.

Likewise if you need to motivate yourself to go to the gym at the end of an exhausting workday, "Focus on the benefits": Think about the wonderful things that being fit enables you to do—and that you will do—from feeling healthy and being energetic when you wake in the mornings, to looking great in your suit or dress or swimwear, to skiing with your children when you're eighty.

This technique does not make every effort a breeze; that's not the point. The point is that when we have to do difficult things that are good for our lives, we need to use the best tools we have to motivate ourselves to act. One of the best tools we have toward this end is our love of our values. Motivating ourselves by appealing to them works. The secret to making this technique work is to visualize the benefits as vividly as possible. Try it. You'll be surprised how well it works.

One more vital principle I use is what I call *the 100 percent rule*: One hundred percent of the shots you don't take won't go in. (This is adapted from hockey player Wayne Gretzky's great line, "You miss 100 percent of the shots you don't take.")

I discovered this gem when I was single, and I applied it, among other ways, to various aspects of the process of seeking a great girl—and it worked. One hundred percent of the girls you don't ask out won't go out with you. But the principle applies to pretty much everything: One hundred percent of the schools you don't apply to won't accept you. One hundred percent of the business plans you don't create won't be funded. One hundred percent of the articles you don't write won't be published. One hundred percent of the scuba lessons you don't take won't move you closer to swimming through underwater worlds of wonder. One hundred percent of the flights you don't book won't take you to Italy. And so on. In every case, although taking action might not guarantee that you will get the value, it markedly increases your chances—and not taking action guarantees that you won't get the value.

(For more of these kinds of highly practical principles and standing orders, see *Thinking in Principles*.)

Living *fully* purposefully means deciding what you truly selfishly want in each of the major areas of your life—and all of the lesser areas, too—figuring out what you need to do to get them, and going after them as if you live only once, because you do. It means filling every moment of your life with the pursuit of conscious, intentional, self-serving goals. It means being fully selfish as a matter of unwavering principle.

Is this easy? No. But you now have a few more vital tools toward that end—and the incentive couldn't be better. Get busy living.

8

Egoism, Benevolence, and Generosity

Can we gain selfish, life-serving values by engaging in acts of benevolence or generosity?

That question might strike you as ridiculous. *Of course* such acts can be in our self-interest. If we look at our lives and the lives of other people, we can see countless instances of people reaping life-serving benefits by being kind or generous: You hold the door for someone; he or she says, "thank you"; you feel good for having been kind. You feed your neighbor's cat while he's away; he's appreciative; you're happy to have helped. You mentor a young entrepreneur and provide guidance that augments his success; he's grateful; you're delighted. We could multiply such examples endlessly.

But the mere fact that an act of benevolence or generosity makes us feel good does not mean that it is in our self-interest. An altruist "feels good" about selflessly serving others—because he has accepted the notion that doing so makes him "moral"—yet doing so is actually bad for his life. Even a committed egoist can feel good about what amounts to a selfless act of benevolence or generosity—if he doesn't understand why it is selfless. For instance, he might cheerfully donate to a charitable organization such as Greenpeace, whose mission includes destroying values on which human flourishing depends, such as the fossil fuel industry.[1]

Not all acts of benevolence and generosity are self-interested.

The objective standard for assessing such acts is not our feelings but the factual requirements of our life and happiness. And understanding how that standard applies to such acts is crucially important on two counts: First, knowing clearly, in terms of principle, when such acts are self-interested and when they are not enables us to act *consistently* selfishly in this area and thus to flourish all the more; second, such understanding fortifies our ability to champion rational egoism and to defend this vital morality against those who misrepresent and demonize it. So let's proceed to identify the relevant principles.

Benevolence is the act of being kind or considerate. And generosity is the act of giving more than the recipient has reason to expect or a right to demand.[2]

Right off the bat we can see that such actions are not universally in accordance with the requirements of human life; thus they are not egoistic virtues per se. Whereas it is always selfish to be rational, honest, and just, it is not always selfish to be benevolent or generous; it depends on the context.[3] Being kind to a known rapist, murderer, or jihadist would be immoral (unless you're feigning kindness to capture him, thwart his efforts, infiltrate his group, or the like). And being generous to such a creature would be even worse.

But being kind or generous to people we know to be morally good—or at least have no reason to regard as morally bad—*can* be in our self-interest and indeed *is* in our self-interest when doing so is in accordance with our rational, life-based hierarchy of values.[4]

We'll focus first on benevolence.

Selfish Benevolence

Consider a few simple instances:

You make your lover a candlelit dinner, put on his (or her) favorite music, and treat him to an evening of bliss; he's elated; you're ecstatic; your relationship strengthens and grows.

You tell your friend that she looks stunning in her new dress; she smiles with delight; you feel happy for her joy; your friendship advances once again.

You compliment your gardener on his artful landscaping; he feels proud; you feel good; your world is better for the exchange.

You tell a coworker how much you appreciate him covering for you when you were ill; he's happy to have helped and appreciative of your appreciation; you both know you'll reciprocate—and you both benefit from the mutual benevolence.

Similar examples abound. And what they collectively show is that, at least on a commonsense level, benevolence toward people we love, care about, or regard as respectable provides us with some kind and degree of life-serving value. Deeper and broader evidence lies ahead, but at this stage we can see that certain acts of benevolence support or lead to life-serving values, good relationships, even sexual ecstasy. Not a bad start.

The selfishness involved in being kind or considerate to people we love, care about, or respect, however, is relatively obvious. What about benevolence toward perfect strangers? Where's the selfish value in being kind to a courier who you'll likely never see again? Where's the egoistic return in telling a stranger that his wallet fell to the floor? What's in it for you to let someone pull in front of you in traffic or to give your seat to an elderly stranger in a crowded airport?

Part of the answer to all such questions is simple: It feels good to be kind and considerate, and doing so fosters the kind of world in which we want to live. But feelings are not our means of knowledge and thus are not our proper guide to action; reason is. And although the desire to live in a world where people are generally benevolent makes sense, that desire does not address the question of when acts of kindness are selfish and when they are not. In order to *know* whether an action is right or wrong, selfish or selfless, we have to know whether it is life-serving or life-throttling.

Are there *reasons*—as in *fact-based principles*—by reference to which we can make such assessments? There are.

Toward identifying them inductively, observe some relevant facts and related questions:

Although you may now have friends, you have not always had them. Your friends used to be strangers. How did you meet and befriend them? Did you do so by treating them unkindly or indifferently? Or did you befriend them by treating them kindly and considerately? What would have happened if you had done the former? And why?

Likewise, although you may currently have a job or a career, you've not always had one. In working your way into your job or building your career, did you interact with strangers? If so, how did you treat them—and why—and how did that work out? If you're still working toward a job or career, which approach to dealing with people do you think will best serve your selfish purposes—being generally kind and considerate, or being generally unkind or indifferent?

If you have a boyfriend, girlfriend, or spouse, how did you treat him or her when you first met? How did that work out for you? If you don't have a lover, which approach to dealing with strangers do you think will best serve your rational self-interest—one of general benevolence toward them, or one of general malevolence or apathy?

As we can see by looking at our own lives, a policy of general benevolence toward strangers *has been* and *is* a major life-serving value. Although not every such act leads to friendship, romance, or employment, every such act adds to the amount of benevolence in our world—and entails the possibility of leading to substantial improvements in our lives down the line. (More on that latter point below.)

It is no accident that the countless books that have been written about how to make friends and influence people, how to succeed in romance, how to succeed in business, how to succeed in *life*—all of them, without exception—advise that we treat people kindly. Kindness pays.

And observations to this effect extend far beyond our immediate personal contexts. Every life-serving value ever produced by means of cooperation or teamwork came into existence substantially because the people involved treated each other kindly and considerately.

Could the U.S. founders have created the land of liberty if they had not been generally benevolent toward one another and toward their fellow Americans? Not a chance. How could they have met, befriended one another, and cooperated to the extent that they did? How could they have conceived and drafted the Declaration of Independence, rallied the American people to the cause, and executed and won the war against all odds? How could they have conceived and drafted the U.S. Constitution and established a system of checks and balances and the separation of powers? How could they have done *any* of this if they had been characteristically less than kind and considerate as a matter of course?

This is not to suggest that the founders never quarreled. They quarreled a lot. But arguing is not the same thing as being unkind or inconsiderate. Nor were the founders always kind. Some of them were, on occasion, downright nasty to each other. But all of that is beside the point. Had the founders been *generally* unkind or indifferent to one another or to their fellow Americans—had they done so *characteristically, as a matter of course*—the United States would never have come to be. People simply cannot cooperate under such conditions.

Could John D. Rockefeller have developed his oil-refining technologies, created Standard Oil, and thereby launched the industry that made possible the modern industrial world if he had been less than kind and considerate to people as a matter of course? No way. Who would have worked for him? With what kind of commitment or diligence would they have worked? Would they have liked their employer? What would the ramifications of *that* have been? This is not to suggest that Rockefeller was always cordial. He was ruthlessly competitive. But that is not the same as unkind. Nor is it to suggest that he was always kind. Perhaps he was not. But had Rockefeller been *characteristically* unkind or indifferent to people, he could not have succeeded in his efforts and thus would not have improved our world as he did. Complex and sustained cooperation and teamwork require kindness and considerateness.

Could Norman Borlaug have saved more than a billion people from starvation—as he did by means of his revolutionary work in biotechnology and agriculture—if he had been generally unkind or indifferent to people? Who would have worked for him? What would have motivated *him* to do the work? Could Maria Montessori have experimented sufficiently in classrooms to develop her profoundly life-serving educational method if she had been malevolent or apathetic toward her students and their parents? Could Willis Carrier have invented and manufactured the modern air conditioner . . . Could Henry Ford have developed his efficient and effective assembly line . . . Could Louis Pasteur have discovered the principles of microbiology, vaccination, and pasteurization . . . Could Thomas Edison, the Wright brothers, Sam Walton, Walt Disney, Steve Jobs, Jeff Bezos, Richard Branson, Joss Whedon, Lin-Manuel Miranda, or any other great producer of life-serving values that require cooperation have succeeded in his work if he had treated people poorly as a matter of course?

None of this is to suggest that great producers never treat people poorly. Some occasionally do. Nor is it to suggest that characteristically unkind people never accomplish anything of value. Perhaps some do (though I'm drawing a blank on that one). Rather, the point is that kindness and considerateness are key ingredients in the human relationships and joint ventures that have given rise to major life-serving values throughout history—and in the absence of a generally benevolent attitude toward others, many of the great producers who have rained values on the world and riches on themselves would not and could not have done so.

This is why companies such as Google, Amazon, and Apple explicitly look for kindness and considerateness in prospective hires, and seek to foster such characteristics in their corporate environments. Such companies are, of course, extremely demanding of their employees, but demanding is not the same as unkind. Google, for instance, looks for people with "creatively benevolent impulses" that "can be backed up by engineering resources and managerial support." The company needs people who work well together, so, as its senior vice president of people operations explains, "The goal of our interview process is to predict how candidates will perform once they join the team." A prospective hire's intelligence and ability are enormously important to Google, but if the person can't get along well with others, his potential value to the company plummets. "We certainly turn down people who are ridiculously smart, but who won't be collaborative when they get here," explains the company's director of staffing.[5]

By looking at our lives, history, the business world, and reality in general, we can see that benevolence, kindness, and considerateness are part of a psychological substratum on which social harmony, civilized society, and industrial and economic progress depend. Thus, if we value these things, we have reason to champion and uphold the principle of *rational benevolence*: the general truth that people should be kind and considerate toward one another—unless they have specific reason not to be.[6]

That proviso—"unless they have specific reason not to be"—is important and worth emphasizing. If you happen upon a stranger with a swastika tattoo, obviously you should not be kind to him. You should ignore him or, if some form of engagement is unavoidable, engage minimally and flatly. (If you discover some explanatory factor such as that he's in costume for a movie role and the tattoo is fake, you might revise your attitude accordingly.) The proviso is necessary to the objectivity of the principle. But *with* the proviso, the principle is rock solid. As a general rule, the standing order to treat people kindly (unless we have specific reason not to) is a policy of rational self-interest. This will become even clearer as we proceed.

So far we've focused only on the *benefits* of benevolence, which we've found to be massive. Now let's consider the *costs*.

Again, we'll begin with a few simple examples:

You hold a door for someone; it takes a few seconds; he says "thank you" or nods in appreciation. The cost: a few seconds of your time—which you are likely to recoup when someone holds a door for you down the line.

You say a kind "hello" to a barista; you ask how her day is going, or remark on her pretty glasses; you order a coffee and tip her for her friendly, helpful service; she feels good, you feel good, kindness and goodwill expand in your world. The cost: a pittance.

A skier wipes out and ends up several yards downhill from his skis; you stop, collect his skis, and carry them down to him; he's thankful; you're happy to have helped; benevolence infuses the day. The cost: a minute and a few calories—both of which you're almost certain to recoup next time you take such a spill.

Again, such examples abound. And what they collectively demonstrate is that the time and effort required to be kind and considerate are scant relative to the values we gain thereby.

But there's more. Oftentimes such minor acts of benevolence that cost us little or nothing amount to the beginnings of major relationships that improve our lives dramatically. Suppose you get to know that barista and the two of you fall in love, or start a business together, or become tennis partners, or all of the above—or more? This kind of thing happens all the time—but only to people who are kind and considerate.

Suppose you get to know the person you help with his skis, and it turns out that he's an executive at Google or Penguin or Cirque du Soleil—and he offers you a job, contract, or audition that launches your career? Again, this kind of thing happens all the time—but only to people who engage in such benevolence.

We could go on. But the point is clear: Given the massive benefits and minuscule costs of benevolence, the standing order to be kind to strangers (unless we have specific reason not to) makes perfect, egoistic sense.

Consider, in this connection, the so-called waiter rule, which points to a related matter of special interest to rational egoists. As humorist Dave Barry famously put it: "A person who is nice to you, but rude to the waiter, is not a nice person."[7] That's generally true, and the principle involved is broader and deeper than Barry's memorable quip suggests.

Assuming the waiter in question has done nothing to deserve such poor treatment, why on earth would someone be rude to him? Almost invariably, when someone is rude for no good reason, it is due to a lack of self-esteem.

A person with high self-esteem has it because he has exerted the thought and effort necessary to show himself that he is able to deal with reality (hence his self-confidence) and worthy of success and happiness (hence his self-respect). Consequently, he sees himself as efficacious, he sees the world as amenable to his success, and he sees other people as potential if not actual values. His corresponding policy is precisely the one we have induced as objectively correct: He exudes general benevolence and goodwill—unless he has specific reason not to.

As Ayn Rand put it: "One of the highest values to a man of reason and self-esteem is other human beings. Of any category in the universe, human beings are of greatest interest to him."

> If he can deal with men of ability, of moral character, of stature—if he can see in other men that which he values, if he can see in them the virtues he creates in himself—then there is a selfish gain to him, on several counts. On the practical level, it is to his advantage to deal with other independent, productive, intelligent men. On the so-called personal level, it is to his advantage to deal with men he can respect and admire.[8]

Because any given stranger could be independent, productive, intelligent, and admirable, a man of reason and self-esteem treats strangers with what Rand called "benevolent neutrality"[9] and "initial good will in the name of their human potential."[10]

People who lack self-esteem (or have low self-esteem) have no such policy—or, if they do have such a policy, they have trouble upholding it. They often treat others poorly because doing so makes them temporarily feel big whereas their lack of self-esteem makes them characteristically feel small. This observation has important implications for egoists, because we don't want to get involved in any substantial way with such people.

Self-esteem is a major indicator of one's psychology, character, and trustworthiness. People who have high self-esteem can make good lovers, good friends, good business partners, good babysitters, even good politicians. People who lack self-esteem (or have low self-esteem) cannot. Of course, anyone can choose to change: A person who lacks self-esteem can choose to begin thinking and acting rationally and thus to raise his self-esteem over time. And if he does, eventually he can join the ranks of the trustworthy. But until he does, egoists should beware.

So we might broaden Dave Barry's idea and call it the "selfish benevolence rule": A person who is unkind to others for no good reason lacks self-esteem; thus, if you must engage with him, beware.

As rational egoists, we want to live in a world where people are kind and considerate unless they have good reason not to be. And we have the best reason in the world to want this: Human beings can be and often are enormous values to us, to our friends, and to our loved ones. Thus treating people kindly unless we have good reason not to—and expecting others to do the same—is a matter of rational self-interest.

Let's set our sights on generosity.

Selfish Generosity

As noted earlier, generosity consists in giving more than the recipient has reason to expect or a right to demand. Specifically, it involves giving a person (or organization) money, time, expertise, information, or some other significant value. When might such an action be in our self-interest? When (a) we regard the recipient as *worthy*—and (b) we see the act of generosity as consistent with our rational hierarchy of values and thus as *non-sacrificial.*

Importantly, being worthy is *not* the same as being entitled. If someone is entitled to something, then giving it to him is not a matter of generosity but a matter of justice and thus a moral imperative. In an act of generosity, the recipient is not owed the assistance; he does not have a moral claim or a right to it. Rather, the giver has determined that from his (the giver's) perspective, the recipient's character, situation, and aims qualify him for the money, time, expertise, or whatever the giver is offering.[11]

Thus, whether a potential recipient is worthy of generosity depends not only on what he has done or seeks to do, but also on the giver's context, values, and aims.

Do you value a cure for cancer? If so, then contributing to an individual or organization dedicated to curing cancer might be in your self-interest. It depends: Do you regard the person or organization as worthy? And, given your value hierarchy, would the contribution be non-sacrificial?

Do you value economic education? If so, then contributing to an individual or organization dedicated to providing such education might be in your self-interest—again, depending on whether you regard the recipient as worthy, and whether the assistance would be non-sacrificial.

Do you value Shakespearean theater, or technologies that enable the disabled, or the spread of rational philosophy? If so, then contributing to individuals or organizations that produce or advance such values might be in your self-interest—depending on your answers to the two key questions.

If and when we regard both the recipient as worthy and the aid as non-sacrificial, then our choice to be generous is rationally selfish.

Of course, determining whether a potential recipient is worthy and whether the aid in question would be non-sacrificial is not always easy. Indeed, it can be extremely difficult because the context can be highly complex. Even a decision about something as seemingly straightforward as whether to help a friend move into a new apartment this weekend can involve significant complexity: What is the context? How good a friend is he? Is he the kind of friend who reciprocates? Or is he the kind who takes but never gives? What are your other possible uses of the time and energy this project would require? Do you already have plans for the weekend? If so, how important are they? Does it even make sense for your friend to do such heavy lifting and to ask for such help from friends? Is he a financially poor student? Is he a wealthy businessman? If the former, it might make sense. If the latter, you might suggest that he hire a moving company to do the bulk of the work, so the two of you can brainstorm about a new productivity app or play golf or do something more enjoyable than cart heavy furniture and big boxes.

Likewise for decisions about whether contributing to a given charity is in your self-interest. Should you donate to the children's hospital? What's the context? How much do you value what this hospital does? What's its mission? What's its track record? Has it spent its funding efficiently and effectively in the past? Has it carried out its stated mission and met or exceeded expectations? What are its future plans? What other organizations have a similar mission? What are *their* track records and plans? And so on.

The complexity that can attend such decisions highlights the importance of establishing and maintaining a clear hierarchy of values. If we don't have that hierarchy, we can't think clearly about such matters.[12]

The bottom line is that if we want to ensure that our acts of generosity are genuinely self-interested, we must bring *reason* to bear on the matter. We must consider the full context, refer to our value hierarchy, and apply the principle of non-sacrifice. If, in accordance with all of that, we determine that a given act of generosity is in our self-interest, then it is.[13]

Finally, it is worth emphasizing the role of *spiritual* values and *long-range* thinking in all of this. Our values are not merely physical but also spiritual, and they are not only short range but also long range. Our values—in the form of our aims and concerns—can extend even beyond our lifetime (as any parent, innovator, artist, or intellectual can attest).

Ayn Rand provided an eloquent example of this. When a questioner asked whether her choice to speak at Ford Hall Forum for a meager fee (or perhaps for free) constituted an act of altruism, she replied:

> You assume that the only possible values one can derive from any activity are financial. . . . That's placing your self-interest terribly low and terribly cheap. . . .
>
> Well then what's my purpose? Altruism? No. In any proper deal, you act on the trader principle—you give a value, and you receive a value. Your question would imply that . . . unless I am paid, I have no interest in spreading ideas which I believe to be right and true, that the only purpose is to enlighten others. That would mean that I have no interest in a free society, I have no interest in

> denouncing the kind of evil which I can see and want to speak against—that all [of] that is *not* to my selfish interest, that it's only to the interest of my audience but not to mine. That would be an impossible contradiction. If I believed it, I wouldn't be worth two cents as a speaker. . . .
>
> I have the most profound and the most selfish interest in having the freedom of my mind, knowing what to do with it, and therefore fighting to preserve it in the country for as long as I am alive—or even beyond my life. I don't care about posterity, but I *do* care about any free mind or any independent person that may be born in future centuries. I do care about them.[14]

On examination, we can see that, although benevolence and generosity are not moral virtues per se, they can be, and often are, profoundly selfish.

9

Ayn Rand's Theory of Rights: The Moral Foundation of a Free Society

What are rights? Where do they come from? One's answers to these questions determine whether one is capable of defending a free society. If one does not know the nature and source of rights, one cannot know whether rights are real or imagined. And if rights are not real, there is no foundation for freedom; governments and societies may do as they please.

The traditional answers to the above questions fall into three categories: (1) Rights are *moral* laws specifying what a person *should* be free to do, and they come from *God*. (2) Rights are *political* laws specifying what a person *is* free to do, and they are created by *governments*. (3) Rights are *moral* laws specifying what a person *should* be free to do, and they are *inherent in man's nature*. But each of these theories is demonstrably false, and a person or society attempting to defend freedom on such grounds will ultimately fail—as Americans are failing today.

Ayn Rand's answers to the above questions, however, are demonstrably true—and those who come to understand her answers thereby equip themselves to defend freedom on solid, philosophic ground.

Toward understanding Rand's theory of rights and its crucial value in the cause of freedom, let us begin with a brief overview of the traditional theories and their essential deficiencies. Then we will turn to Rand's theory, see how it solves the various problems left unsolved by the other theories, and discover how it grounds rights in observable facts.

Traditional Theories of Rights and Why They Are Wrong

God-Given Rights

The idea that rights come from God is particularly popular among conservatives and Republicans. According to this theory, an all-powerful, infallible, all-good being makes moral law and gives man rights; thus rights exist prior to and apart from any man-made law and cannot be granted or repealed by government. As Sarah Palin puts it: "The Constitution didn't give us our rights. Our rights came from God, and they're inalienable. The Constitution created a national government to protect our God-given, unalienable rights."[1] Rush Limbaugh agrees: "You have individual rights, as granted by God, who created you, and our founding documents enshrine them: Life, liberty, pursuit of happiness. Those rights don't come from other men or governments. . . . They come from our Creator."[2] Newt Gingrich challenges anyone to identify another possible source of inalienable rights: "If you are not endowed by your Creator with certain inalienable rights where do they come from?"[3] And James Dobson warns: "If you say that rights do not come from God, and they come from the state, they can be taken away."[4]

But the theory that rights come from God is hopeless. To begin with, there is no evidence for the existence of such a being, much less for the existence of rights that somehow emanate from his will. Whether one believes in God is beside the point here. Either way, the fact remains that there is no evidence for God's existence, which is why it is supposed to be accepted on faith—in the *absence* of evidence. Rights in support of which there is no evidence are not rights but fantasies.

Further, what would it mean for an all-powerful, infallible, and all-good being to give man rights? Surely, if God existed and possessed such qualities, he could at any time repeal those rights and kill people at will (as he does in the stories of the Old Testament) or command or permit certain people to kill, enslave, or rape others (as he does in the scriptures of Judaism, Christianity, and Islam). And if God—who is supposed to be infallible, all good, and the maker of moral law—did commit or permit such acts, then such acts would, by definition, be morally good. "Rights" that can be revoked are not rights but permissions. And a "theory" of rights that permits murder, enslavement, and rape is not a theory of rights but a mockery of them.

The supposition that rights come from God entails additional problems (e.g., which "God"—Yahweh? Brahman? Allah?), but the foregoing flaws are sufficient to disqualify it. The "theory" amounts not to a rational theory about a demonstrable source of inalienable rights, but to a fantasy about supernatural permissions.

To say that rights come from God is to say that there is no evidence in support of their existence, that there is no basis for them in perceptual reality, that they are not rationally provable. This is not a sound theory of rights; it cannot serve as a solid foundation on which to advocate or defend liberty.

Government-Granted Rights

Leftists and modern "liberals" cash in on this apparent absence of evidence. There is no such thing as rights, they say, at least not in the sense of absolute moral prerogatives to live one's own life, by one's own judgment, in pursuit of one's own happiness. Rights, say the left, do not precede political laws but *follow* from them: Governments create laws, and the laws, in turn, dictate the rights and non-rights of the people who live under those governments. "Absent a government," writes E. J. Dionne, "there are no rights."[5] Stephen Holmes and Cass Sunstein elaborate: "[R]ights are powers granted by the political community"; thus, "an interest qualifies as a right when an effective legal system treats it as such by using collective resources to defend it." Holmes and Sunstein conclude by favorably quoting Utilitarian philosopher Jeremy Bentham, who famously said a "right" is a "child of the law"[6] and thus that "imprescriptible rights" (i.e., inalienable rights) are "rhetorical nonsense, nonsense upon stilts."[7]

Rights, on this account, are governmental decrees: If the government says that you have a right to take a particular action (or to be provided with a particular good or service), then you do; if the government says you don't, then you don't.

But this notion of rights entails a fundamental contradiction. The idea that rights are permissions granted by a government (or a legal system or a political community or the like) contradicts the very *purpose* of the concept of rights. Rights are fundamentally a *moral* concept; they pertain to that which a person *should* be free to do. The essential function of the concept is to specify those actions that no one—including government—can *morally* preclude one from taking. Whether rights actually exist is beside the point here. The purpose of the concept—its function in thought and communication—is to identify the actions (real or imagined) that a person morally must be free to take and to distinguish them from the actions that he morally may be prohibited from taking. To say that rights are governmental decrees is to imply, among other absurdities, that Islamic theocracies do nothing wrong in stoning adulterous women or hanging homosexuals—and that the Nazis did nothing wrong in torturing and killing millions of Jews—because, well, the governments involved deem such people to be right-less.

"Rights" that can be granted or nullified by governments are not rights but political policies (or laws), and they logically should be identified as such. To call them "rights" is to abuse language.[8]

The notion that governments create rights is not a viable foundation on which to advocate or defend liberty.

Natural Rights

Well aware of the dangers of governments dictating what "rights" people have and have not, Enlightenment thinkers, classical liberals, and the Founding Fathers sought to ground rights in *nature*. Rights, they posited, are born not of man-made law but of *natural law*—specifically, natural *moral* law: natural law concerning how people should and should not act. As John Locke put it, there is "a law of nature," and this law "teaches all mankind, who will but consult it, that being all equal and independent, no one ought to harm another in his life, health, liberty, or possessions."[9] The Founders agreed. "Man," wrote Thomas Jefferson, is "endowed by nature with rights,"[10] and these rights are a matter of "moral law";[11] thus they are "inherent," "inalienable," and "unchangeable."[12] A free people claim "their rights as derived from the laws of nature, and not as the gift of their chief magistrate."[13]

This is the view held by many "constitutional conservatives," Tea Partiers, and others who admirably seek to defend freedom. But this theory does not withstand scrutiny, either.

The "natural" law to which Locke, Jefferson, and the other Enlightenment thinkers refer is not natural law but "supernatural" law. It comes not from nature but from "God." As Locke put it in the extended version of the passage quoted above: There is a "law of nature," and this law

> teaches all mankind, who will but consult it, that being all equal and independent, no one ought to harm another in his life, health, liberty, or possessions: for men being all the workmanship of one omnipotent, and infinitely wise maker; all the servants of one sovereign master, sent into the world by his order, and about his business; they are his property, whose workmanship they are, made to last during his, not one another's pleasure.[14]

In other words, the "law of nature" that gives rise to man's rights is the law of God: *He* ordains that we are *his* property and must serve *his* purposes; thus, men may not make us serve *their* purposes.[15]

Jefferson and the other Founders held essentially the same view. "The moral law of our nature," wrote Jefferson, is "the moral law to which man has been subjected by his Creator."[16]

> Under the law of nature, all men are born free, every one comes into the world with a right to his own person, which includes the liberty of moving and using it at his own will. This is what is called personal liberty, and is given him by the Author of nature.[17]

Alexander Hamilton wrote:

> Good and wise men, in all ages . . . have supposed that the deity, from the relations we stand in to himself and to

> each other, has constituted an eternal and immutable law, which is indispensably obligatory upon all mankind, prior to any human institution whatever. This is what is called the law of nature. . . . Upon this law depend the natural rights of mankind.[18]

George Mason wrote: "The laws of nature are the laws of God, Whose authority can be superseded by no power on earth."[19] And John Adams wrote that man possesses rights "antecedent to all earthly government—Rights, that cannot be repealed or restrained by human laws—Rights, derived from the great Legislator of the universe."[20]

This is the generally accepted view of the source and meaning of "natural" rights. But the idea that rights come from a law of nature created by God is beset with all the same problems as the idea that rights come from God—because it is the same idea, albeit with God's involvement one step removed.

If natural rights come from God, then proof of their existence depends on proof of God's existence—and further, on proof that God somehow makes rights exist and cannot repeal them. But, again, there is no evidence for the existence of God, much less for the existence of natural moral laws or inalienable rights that somehow emanate from his will.

To accept the existence of "God" is ultimately to accept it on *faith*; accordingly, to accept the idea that "rights" somehow "come from God" is to rest one's case for rights on faith. This will not do. As Ayn Rand observed:

> [T]o rest one's case on *faith* means to concede . . . that one has no rational arguments to offer . . . that there are no rational arguments to support the American system, no rational justification for freedom, justice, property, individual rights, that these rest on a mystic revelation and

> can be accepted only *on faith*—that in reason and logic the enemy is right.[21]

This is undeniably true.

With all due respect to Locke and the Founders (and the respect due is *monumental*), the idea that rights come from God or from a law of nature created by God not only fails to meet the requirement of demonstrability; it also concedes that reason and logic are on the side of tyrants.

Neither the notion that rights come from God—nor the notion that they come from government—nor the notion that they come from a law of nature created by God is viable. None of these theories identifies a demonstrable, observation-based source for rights. None explains *rationally* why people should be free to live (the right to *life*); to act on their own judgment, free of coercion (*liberty*); to keep, use, and dispose of the product of their effort (*property*); and to pursue the goals and values of their own choosing (*the pursuit of happiness*). None supplies an objective foundation for freedom.

In the absence of demonstrable proof of the existence of rights, proponents of rights have nothing to support their claims—and the modern intellectuals know it. As philosopher Alasdair MacIntyre bluntly and mockingly puts it:

> [T]hose rights which are alleged to belong to human beings as such and which are cited as a reason for holding that people ought not to be interfered with in their pursuit of life, liberty and happiness. . . . the rights which are spoken of in the eighteenth century as natural rights or as the rights of man. . . . there are no such rights, and belief in them is one with belief in witches and unicorns.
>
> The best reason for asserting so bluntly that there are no such rights is indeed of precisely the same type as the best

> reason which we possess for asserting that there are no witches and the best reason which we possess for asserting that there are no unicorns: every attempt to give good reasons for believing that there *are* such rights has failed.[22]

If we want to defend rights, we need to be able to do more than just *say* that we have them. We need to be able *rationally* to explain where rights come from and why we have them. Toward that end, we need a rational account of natural moral law—moral law derived not from "super-nature" but from *actual*nature—moral law not merely asserted but proven—proven by means of evidence and logic.

Ayn Rand provided just that.

Like Locke and the Founders, Rand held that individuals have a right to life, liberty, property, and the pursuit of happiness. But she arrived at this conclusion in a very different manner than did they or any other natural rights advocates. Whereas traditional conceptions of rights are based (ultimately) on presumptions of God, Rand's conception is rooted in observations of fact. Her theory of rights derives from her more fundamental theory of morality—which derives from her observations of reality, of the nature of values, and of the requirements of life. Thus, to understand Rand's theory of rights, we must begin with a brief survey of her theory of morality and the observable facts that give rise to it.

Ayn Rand's Observation-Based Morality

Our purpose here is not to flesh out Rand's entire moral theory, which would require a book, but rather to examine certain aspects of her ethics that are essential to understanding her theory of rights. Thus, I want to stress that the following streamlined survey is no substitute for a thorough study of her ethics.[23]

Morality or ethics, observed Rand, "is a code of values to guide man's choices and actions—the choices and actions that determine the purpose and the course of his life."[24] And the first step toward understanding a *code* of values, she reasoned, is to understand the *nature* of values. Thus, Rand's approach to morality began not with the question: Which of the existing codes should I accept?—but rather with the questions: "What are *values*? Why does man need them?"[25] These questions directed her thinking away from the established views and toward the facts of reality.

Looking at reality, Rand observed that a "value" is "that which one acts to gain and/or keep."[26] We can see the truth of this all around us: People act to gain and keep money; they value money. Students act to gain and keep good grades; they value good grades. Churchgoers act to gain or keep a relationship with "God"; they value that relationship. People act to develop fulfilling careers, to establish and maintain romantic relationships, to gain and keep freedom, and so on. The things one acts to gain or keep are one's values. And the key word here is: *acts*. Values are objects of *actions*. (Please take special note of this, as it is a crucial aspect of Rand's derivation of moral principles—including the principle of rights. We will observe the relationship of actions and values repeatedly and with mounting significance throughout the remainder of this essay.)

Looking at reality, Rand further saw that this phenomenon involves not only human beings but *all*living things—and *only* living things. We can see this: Trees, tigers, and people take actions toward goals. Rocks, rivers, and hammers do not. Trees, for example, extend their roots into the ground and their branches and leaves toward the sky; they value minerals, water, and sunlight. Tigers hunt antelope and nap under trees; they value meat and shade. This pattern continues throughout the plant and animal kingdom: *All living things take self-generated, goal-directed action.*

Nonliving things, on the other hand, take no such action. They can be moved, but they cannot act—not in the self-generated, goal-directed sense that living things do. A rock just remains wherever it is unless some outside force, such as a wave or a hammer, hits and moves it. A river flows, but its motion is not self-generated; water moves only by means of some outside force—in this case, the gravitational pull of the earth. And a hammer does not, by itself, smash rocks or drive nails; it does not generate its own action.

Rand observed that the reason inanimate objects do not act in the same sense that living things do is that they have no needs and therefore no corresponding means of action. Only living organisms have needs, goals, or values; accordingly, only they have a means of acting toward such ends.

Having clarified that a value is that which one acts to gain or keep—and that only living things pursue values—Rand proceeded to ask: *Why* do living things seek values? What are values *for*? "The concept 'value' is not a primary," Rand observed. "It presupposes an answer to the question: of value to *whom*and for *what*? It presupposes an entity capable of acting to achieve a goal in the face of an alternative." A tree faces the alternative of reaching water and sunlight—or not. A tiger faces the alternative of catching and keeping its prey—or not. And a person faces the alternative of achieving *his* goals—or not. The objects a living thing acts to gain or keep are *its* values—values *to it*.

That answers the question: "to whom?" But the question "for what?" remains.

What *difference* does it make whether an organism achieves its goals? What happens if it succeeds? What happens if it fails? What *ultimately* is at stake? Here is Rand's key passage on the issue:

> There is only one fundamental alternative in the universe: existence or non-existence—and it pertains to a single class of entities: to living organisms. The existence of inanimate matter is unconditional, the existence of life is not: it depends on a specific course of action. Matter is indestructible, it changes forms, but it cannot cease to exist. It is only a living organism that faces a constant alternative: the issue of life or death. Life is a process of self-sustaining and self-generated action. If an organism fails in that action, it dies; its chemical elements remain, but its life goes out of existence.[27]

The reason why living things need values is: to *live*. The answer to the question "for *what*?" is: for *life*. Life is conditional: If a living thing takes the actions necessary to remain alive, it remains alive; if, for whatever reason, it fails to take those actions, it dies. And human beings are no exception to this principle. People need values for the same reason plants and animals do: in order to sustain and further their life.

On the basis of such observations, Rand discovered that an organism's life is its ultimate value and thus its *standard* of value—the standard by which all of its other values and actions are to be evaluated. A tree's standard of value is the requirements of its life as set by *its* nature. A tiger's standard of value is the requirements of its life as set by *its* nature. And a man's standard of value is the requirements of his life as set by *his* nature.

Now, our purpose here is not to examine every nuance of the proof that an organism's life is its standard of value, nor to address every objection that might be raised to the idea.[28] Rather, our purpose is to survey the *essential* facts that give rise to the principle, to see generally how they anchor it in perceptual reality, and ultimately to see how this principle underlies and gives rise to the principle of rights. Toward that end, we will focus on a few crucial components.

By pursuing the question "Why does man need values?" Rand kept her thinking *fact-oriented*. If man needs values, then the *reason* he needs them will go a long way toward establishing which values are legitimate and which are not. If man doesn't need values, well, then, he doesn't need them—and there is no point in pursuing the issue at all.[29] Rand discovered that man *does* need values, and the reason he needs them is in order to *live*. Moral values—values in the realm of human *choice*—are facts in relation to the requirements of man's life.

Because we possess free will, we choose our values; thus, we *can* choose either objectively legitimate, life-serving values (e.g., to pursue a wonderful career, to remain with a worthy spouse, to establish and maintain a civilized society)—or objectively illegitimate, life-thwarting values (e.g., to shoot heroin, to stay with an abusive spouse, or to advocate communism or sharia). But whatever our choices, these facts remain: The only reason we *can* pursue values is because we are alive, and the only reason we *need* to pursue values is in order to live. This observation-based, two-pronged principle is essential to understanding how morality—and, in turn, the principle of rights—is grounded in the immutable facts of reality: Only life makes values *possible*, and only life makes values *necessary*. Or: We have to *be alive* in order to pursue values, and we have to pursue values in order to *stay alive*.

These are metaphysically given facts—facts about the fundamental nature of reality, about how the world is regardless of what anyone hopes, feels, prays, or chooses. And they give rise to a crucial epistemological principle—a principle pertaining to the correct and incorrect use of the concept of "value." Quoting Rand:

> Metaphysically, *life* is the only phenomenon that is an end in itself: a value gained and kept by a constant process of action. Epistemologically, the concept of "value" is genetically dependent upon and derived from the antecedent concept of "life." To speak of "value" as apart from "life" is worse than a contradiction in terms. "It is only the concept of 'Life' that makes the concept of 'Value' possible."[30]

The reason that to speak of value as apart from life is worse than a contradiction in terms is that to do so is to tear the concept of value away from its conceptual foundation—the foundation on which it hierarchically depends and in relation to which it has objective meaning. Ripped away from the concept of life, the concept of value has no grounding in reality; it is severed from its factual base and thus amounts to a subjective utterance. To speak of value as apart from life is to commit what Rand called "the fallacy of concept stealing," which consists in using a concept while ignoring or denying a more fundamental concept on which it logically depends.[31]

The concept of value is *rooted in* the concept of life. Value means "that toward which a living thing acts." And *moral* value—value proper to human beings—means "that toward which a person acts in accordance with the requirements of human life."

Rand further observed that because human beings are individuals—each with his own body, his own mind, his own life—this standard applies to human beings as individuals. Man's life is the standard of moral value—and each individual's *own* life is his *own* ultimate value. Each individual is morally an end in himself—not a means to the ends of others.[32] The moral principle here is *egoism*.

Egoism is the recognition of the fact that each individual should act to promote his own life and is the proper beneficiary of his own moral action.[33] The validity of this principle is implicit in the very *nature* of values. A value is the object of an action taken by a living organism to sustain and further *its*life. Again, the fact that people can choose antilife values doesn't change the roots of the concept of value or the fact that the only demonstrably legitimate values are those that promote one's life.

Importantly, egoism (properly understood) is *not* hedonism or subjectivism; it does not hold "pleasure" or "feelings" as the standard of value. A person may find *pleasure* in actions that are not good for his life; for instance, a ballerina might enjoy eating lots of cake and ice cream, but if doing so causes her to gain too much weight, it will ruin her career as a ballerina. Likewise, a person may *feel*like doing something that is not good for his life; for instance, a salesman might feel like sleeping in one morning, but if doing so means missing a crucial meeting and losing a major customer, it is not in his best interest to do so.

Looking at reality, Rand saw that although experiencing pleasure—and, more broadly, achieving happiness—are crucial aspects of human life, they are not and cannot be the standard of moral value. "Happiness," observed Rand, "can properly be the purpose of ethics, but not the standard. The task of ethics is to define man's proper code of values and thus to give him the means of achieving happiness." She elaborated on the relationship as follows:

> The maintenance of life and the pursuit of happiness are not two separate issues. To hold one's own life as one's ultimate value, and one's own happiness as one's highest purpose are two aspects of the same achievement. Existentially, the activity of pursuing rational goals is the activity of maintaining one's life; psychologically, its result, reward and concomitant is an emotional state of happiness. . . .

> But the relationship of cause to effect cannot be reversed. It is only by accepting "man's life" as one's primary and by pursuing the rational values it requires that one can achieve happiness—not by taking "happiness" as some undefined, irreducible primary and then attempting to live by its guidance. If you achieve that which is the good by a rational standard of value, it will necessarily make you happy; but that which makes you happy, by some undefined emotional standard, is not necessarily the good.[34]

On the basis of such observations, Rand arrived at and validated the dual principle that man's life is the objective standard of moral value, and the achievement of happiness is the moral purpose of each individual's life.

This brings us to the question: How can we know which actions will serve our life and happiness? What must we do to live and prosper? To answer this question, Rand again looked at reality and formulated principles on the basis of observation.

Rand saw that man, like all living things, has a *means* of survival. Whereas plants survive by means of an automatic *vegetative* process (photosynthesis), and whereas animals survive by means of automatic *instinctive* processes (hunting, fleeing, nest-building, etc.), man survives by *volitional* means—by *choosing* to use his mind to identify and pursue the requirements of his life.

While the choice of whether to use one's mind is up to the individual (one can choose to exert mental effort or not to do so), the basic requirements of man's life are set by his nature. They are metaphysically given facts. We need food, clothing, shelter, medicine, and other material goods in order to live and prosper. We also need self-confidence, personal goals, romantic love, and other spiritual values in order to thrive. More fundamentally, we need *knowledge* of such needs and *knowledge* of how to acquire them. So the question becomes: What must we do to gain such knowledge and acquire such values?

Rand observed that first and foremost we must use *reason*, the faculty that identifies and integrates the material provided by man's senses. Reason is our means of understanding the world, ourselves, and our needs; thus, if we want to gain such understanding, we must use it; we must observe reality and think.

> Man cannot survive, as animals do, by the guidance of mere percepts. A sensation of hunger will tell him that he needs food (if he has learned to identify it as "hunger"), but it will not tell him how to obtain his food and it will not tell him what food is good for him or poisonous. He cannot provide for his simplest physical needs without a process of thought. He needs a process of thought to discover how to plant and grow his food or how to make weapons for hunting. His percepts might lead him to a cave, if one is available—but to build the simplest shelter, he needs a process of thought. No percepts and no "instincts" will tell him how to light a fire, how to weave cloth, how to forge tools, how to make a wheel, how to make an airplane, how to perform an appendectomy, how to produce an electric light bulb or an electronic tube or a cyclotron or a box of matches. Yet his life depends on such knowledge—and only a volitional act of his consciousness, a process of thought, can provide it.[35]

And reason is not only our means of gaining knowledge of our *physical* needs; it is also our means of gaining knowledge of our *spiritual* needs. It is by means of reason that we learn what self-confidence is, why we need it, and how to gain it; the importance of long-range goals, which ones will serve our life and happiness, and which ones will not; the nature of love, and how to build and maintain a wonderful romantic relationship; and so on. We are not born with any such knowledge; if and to the extent that we gain it, we do so by means of reason.

On the basis of such observations, Rand identified reason as our fundamental means of living, our basic life-serving value, and thus our basic *moral* value. If we want to live and prosper, we must use reason: We must observe reality and think; we must integrate our observations into concepts, generalizations, and principles that correspond to reality; and we must act accordingly.

Here again is the *action* thread, but now with another element folded in: Whereas all living things must act in order to live, human beings must act *rationally.* This does not mean we must always be correct or never make errors—that would be an impossible standard. We are neither omniscient nor infallible; our knowledge is limited to whatever we have learned at any given time, and we can err in our thought processes, conclusions, and judgments. This, however, is not a problem, because we can always gain additional knowledge or correct errors by applying or reapplying reason—by looking at reality, integrating our observations into concepts and generalizations, and checking for contradictions in our thinking.

The moral principle is: If we are to live and prosper, we must always act on our *rational* judgment—our basic means of living.[36] And this brings us to the question: What can *stop* us from acting on our judgment?

Looking at reality, Rand observed that the only thing that can stop a person from acting on his judgment is other people; and the only way they can stop him is by means of *physical force.*[37] To see this vividly, suppose you are alone on an island. What can stop you from acting on your judgment? Nothing can. If you decide that you should go fishing or pick some berries or build a shelter, you are free to do so. But suppose another person rows up to the island, hops off his boat, and ties you to a tree. Clearly, you are no longer free to act on your judgment. If you had planned to go fishing, you can't go. If you had planned to build a shelter, you can't build it. Whatever your plans were, they are now ruined, and, if you are not freed from bondage, you will soon die.

The brute's force has come between your thinking and your acting, between your planning and your doing. You can no longer act on your judgment; you can no longer act as your life requires; you can no longer live as a human being. Of course, the brute could feed you and keep you breathing; but a "life" of bondage is not a human life. *A human life is a life guided by the judgment of one's mind.*

In order to live as a human being, a person must be able to act on his own judgment; the only thing that can stop him from doing so is other people; and the only way they can stop him is by means of physical force.

This principle holds regardless of location, regardless of the kind of force used (a gun to the head, fraud, the threat of incarceration, etc.), regardless of who uses the force (an individual, a group, or a government), and regardless of the extent to which force is used. A few examples will bear this out.

Suppose a woman is walking to the store intent on using her money to buy groceries, and a thug jumps out from an alley, puts a gun to her head, and says, "Give me your purse or die." Now the woman can't act according to her plan. Either she is going to give her purse to the thief, or she is going to get shot in the head. Either way, she's not going grocery shopping. If she hands her purse to the thief, and if he flees without shooting her, she can resume acting on her judgment—but, importantly, *not* with respect to the stolen money. Although the thief is gone, the effect of his force remains. By keeping the woman's money, he continues to prevent her from spending it, and, *to that extent*, he continues to stop her from acting on her judgment. This ongoing force does not thwart her life totally, but it does thwart her life partially: If she had her money, she would either spend it or save it; but because the thief has her money, she can do neither. She cannot use her money as she chooses, and her life is, to that extent, retarded.

To whatever *degree* physical force is used against a person, it impedes his ability to act on his judgment, his basic means of living.

Take another example. Suppose a man reads an advertisement for a used car and goes to check it out. The owner assures the man that the car's odometer reading is correct; this, however, is not true, and the owner knows it because he turned back the mileage himself. As far as the man can tell, though, the owner is being honest, and everything seems to be in order; so he buys the car and drives it away. But notice that the man is *not* driving the car he bargained for; he is not driving the car he was *willing* to buy. Unbeknownst to him, he is driving a different car—one with higher mileage than the one for which he was willing to pay. By lying to the man about the car's mileage and by selling it to him on the basis of that false information, the crook has defrauded the man. Because the man's willingness to exchange his money for the car was based partly on the crook's lie, the crook has gained and is now keeping the man's money against his will. In so doing, the crook is physically forcing the man to act against his judgment. By fraudulently taking and keeping the man's money, the crook is physically preventing him from spending or saving it as he otherwise would.

Fraud, the act of gaining or keeping someone's property by means of deception, is a form of indirect physical force. It *is* physical force, because, although indirect, it physically impedes the victim's ability to act fully on his judgment. Other types of indirect physical force include *extortion*, the act of gaining or keeping someone's property by distant threat of force; *copyright and patent infringements*, acts of misusing someone's intellectual property (and thus impinging on his ability to act on it); *slander*, the act of making false statements that damage a person's reputation (and thereby retarding his ability to act on it); *unilateral breach of contract*, the act of refusing to deliver goods or services one has agreed to deliver; and so forth. In all such cases, although the force is indirect, it is still physical: When and to the degree it is used, it physically prevents the victim from acting according to his judgment.

Whether direct or indirect, physical force used against a person stops him from living fully as a human being: To the extent it is used, it prevents him from employing his means of survival—the judgment of his mind.

Importantly, lone thugs and crooks are not the only perpetrators of physical force; nor are they the most dangerous. As history makes clear, the most dangerous agents of force, by far, are governments. "A government," observed Rand, "holds a legal monopoly on the use of physical force."

> No individual or private group or private organization has the legal power to initiate the use of physical force against other individuals or groups and to compel them to act against their own voluntary choice. Only a government holds that power. The nature of governmental action is: *coercive* action. The nature of political power is: the power to force obedience under threat of physical injury—the threat of property expropriation, imprisonment, or death.[38]

Everyone today knows that governments such as Nazi, communist, and theocratic regimes have tortured, slaughtered, and otherwise ruined the lives of hundreds of millions of people (and counting). A person forced by a government into a eugenics lab or a concentration camp cannot live as a human being, because he cannot act on the judgment of his mind. A person forced by a government to become a farmer or a dancer or a physicist cannot live as a human being, because he cannot act on his judgment. And a woman forced by a government to wear a burka or to stay with her husband or to stay at home cannot live as a human being, because she cannot act on hers.

But governments can and unfortunately do use physical force against people in subtler, less-obvious ways as well.

Consider, for instance, Anna Tomalis of Clarksville Maryland. In 2004, when Anna was ten years old, she was diagnosed with a rare form of liver cancer. After surgery and chemotherapy failed to halt the cancer, her doctors told her there was nothing more they could do. So Anna and her parents searched the web and discovered experimental drugs that, in clinical trials, had extended the lives of patients with the same kind of cancer. Anna and her parents were relieved: In their judgment, these experimental drugs were worth the risks involved in her taking them.

But the U.S. government forbade the dying girl to take the drugs because the Food and Drug Administration (FDA) hadn't approved them. Asked in an interview what she thought about this situation, Anna replied: "I know there are other drugs out there for me. I'm not happy with it. I don't think it's right." Anna's mother pleaded with Congress to pass a proposed bill that would have enabled Anna to take the drugs: "Please help her. She wants to survive."[39] But Congress did not pass the bill.

Anna wrote to the FDA requesting a "compassionate-use exemption," which, if granted, would permit her to take the drugs. But the FDA bureaucrats took their time. Months passed before they reviewed Anna's request and granted her permission. By then it was too late. Although the drugs might have saved or extended Anna's life if she had been free to take them earlier, at this point the cancer had spread too far, and the drugs could not stop it. After receiving only one round of treatment, she died of the disease. She was then thirteen.

The issue of people being forced to act against their judgment is a matter of life and death. In some cases, such force results in a subhuman existence. In other cases, it means going out of existence. In all cases, it thwarts people's basic means of living and thus stops them from living fully as human beings.

Consider a few more of the countless instances of force used against Americans on a daily basis. We are saddled with laws that force everyone to purchase health insurance (ObamaCare), laws that force bankers to lend money to people they deem un-credit-worthy (Community Reinvestment Act), laws that force citizens to bail out bankers who go bankrupt (TARP), laws that force homeowners to hand over their property for the "greater good" (eminent domain), laws that forbid businessmen from merging their companies (antitrust), laws that forbid couriers from delivering mail (postal monopoly), laws that force people to pay for the education of other people's children (government-run schools), laws that force younger Americans to pay for the health care and retirement of older Americans (Medicare and Social Security), laws that force students to "volunteer" in their communities, laws that forbid employers and employees from contracting in accordance with their own judgment (minimum wage laws), laws that force automakers to "contract" with labor unions on terms that are detrimental to their businesses (National Labor Relations Act)—and on and on. In all such cases, people are forced to act against their own judgment—against their basic means of living; thus they are unable to live fully as human beings.

Of course, people can remain *alive* under these kinds and degrees of force; but insofar as *any* force is used against them, they cannot live *fully* as human beings. A human life *is* a life guided by the judgment of one's mind.

On the basis of such observations, Ayn Rand established the *objective*, fact-based case for individual rights.

Ayn Rand's Observation-Based Principle of Rights

Rand reasoned that because man's life is the standard of moral value, because each person should act to sustain and further his own life, and because physical force used against a person stops him from acting on his basic means of living, we need a moral principle to protect ourselves from people and governments that attempt to use force against us. That principle involves the concept of *rights.*

> "Rights" are a *moral* concept—the concept that provides a logical transition from the principles guiding an individual's actions to the principles guiding his relationship with others—the concept that preserves and protects individual morality in a social context—the link between the moral code of a man and the legal code of a society, between ethics and politics. *Individual rights are the means of subordinating society to moral law.*[40]

The moral law that Rand speaks of here is the principle of egoism—the observation-based moral truth that each individual should act to promote his own life and is the proper beneficiary of his own actions. Individual rights are the means of subordinating society to the *truth* of egoism.

A "right," Rand continues, "is a moral principle defining and sanctioning a man's freedom of action in a social context."[41] Again, the key word is *action.* Just as on the personal level we need principles of action to guide us in pursuing our life-serving values, so on the social level we need principles of *interaction* to protect us from those who attempt to interfere with our plans.

And just as our ultimate value is our own life, so our fundamental right is our right to our own life.

> There is only *one* fundamental right (all others are its consequences or corollaries): a man's right to his own life. Life is a process of self-sustaining and self-generated action; the right to life means the right to engage in self-sustaining and self-generated action—which means: the freedom to take all the actions required by the nature of a rational being for the support, the furtherance, the fulfillment and the enjoyment of his own life. (Such is the meaning of the right to life, liberty and the pursuit of happiness.)[42]

Note Rand's reference to the observable fact that life is a process of self-sustaining and self-generated action. Again, this is a metaphysically given fact; it's the way the world *is*, regardless of what anyone hopes, feels, prays, or does. Life *depends* on such action—and *human* life depends on *rational* action, action in accordance with one's own judgment. Because each individual's life requires self-generated, goal-directed action in accordance with his own judgment, each individual *morally* must be left free to act on his own judgment—and each individual *morally* must leave others free to act on theirs.

Rand further observed that because a right is a sanction to *action*, it is not and cannot be a sanction to be *given* goods or services. If a person had a "right" to be given food, or a house, or medical care, or an education, or the like, that would imply that other people must be *forced* to provide him with these goods or services. It would mean that some people must produce while others dispose of their product. As Rand put it: "The man who produces while others dispose of his product is a slave."

> If some men are entitled by right to the products of the work of others, it means that those others are deprived of

> rights and condemned to slave labor. Any alleged "right" of one man which necessitates the violation of the rights of another, is not and cannot be a right. No man can have a right to impose an unchosen obligation, an unwarranted duty or an involuntary servitude on another man. There can be no such thing as "*the right to enslave*."[43]

The North fought (and thankfully won) a vital war against the South on the principle that there can be no such thing as the right to enslave. Rand made explicit the fundamental reason this principle is *true*. The reason each individual's life should *legally* belong to him is that each individual's life does in fact*morally* belong to him. Each individual is morally an end in himself—not a means to the ends of others. Each individual has a moral right to act on his own judgment for his own sake—and to keep, use, and dispose of the product of his effort—so long as he respects the same right of others.

This brings us to the question: What binds a person to respect the rights of others? Again, Rand's answer is derived from observable facts—many of which we have seen in this essay (and others of which may be seen in a fleshed-out presentation of the morality of egoism).

In essence, what obligates a person to respect the rights of others is his own self-interest. If a person wants to live and be happy, he must recognize and respect the metaphysically given facts of reality (e.g., the fact that everything, including man, has a specific nature), the nature of man (i.e., the kind of being he is), the basic requirements of human life and happiness (e.g., reason, short- and long-term goals, self-esteem), and the social conditions that make peaceful human coexistence possible (e.g., individual rights, freedom, the rule of law).

Granted, although this truth is based on observation and logic, it is nevertheless highly abstract; to grasp it one must exert substantial mental effort—and not everyone will choose to exert that effort. But the abstract nature of a truth does not alter its truth. Just as the abstract nature of the principles of physics and biology does not change the fact that those principles are true, so, too, the abstract nature of the principles of morality does not change the fact that these principles are true. Just as driving one's car off a cliff or failing to treat one's cancer will have a negative effect on one's life regardless of whether one understands the principles involved there, so, too, being irrational or violating rights will have a negative effect on one's life regardless of whether one understands the principles here.

Violating rights does not and cannot lead to happiness; it necessarily retards one's life, leads to unhappiness, and may lead to incarceration or premature death. The evidence of this is all around us: from the "life and happiness" of Bernie Madoff (Wall Street Ponzi-schemer) to that of John Gotti (Mafia "boss"), from the "life and happiness" of Timothy McVeigh (Oklahoma City bomber) to that of Dillon Klebold and Eric Harris (Columbine murderers), from the "life and happiness" of Bashar al-Assad and Mu'ammar Gadhafi to that of sundry swindlers and petty thieves who must constantly worry about being caught, who know that they have chosen to survive not as rational producers but as pathetic parasites on such producers, and whose lives and souls are correspondingly damaged. Protestations to the contrary notwithstanding, these are not happy people.

But even if rights-violators could fool themselves into believing that they are happy (which they can't), the fact remains that by violating the rights of others, they thereby relinquish some or all of their own rights; and rights-respecting people and governments morally may deal with them accordingly. (Rand's views on the nature and need of government and on the proper application of the principle of rights to the various areas of social and political life are a subject for another day. Our concern in this essay is limited to her derivation of and the essential meaning of the principle of rights.)

Respecting the rights of others, observed Rand, "is an obligation imposed, not by the state, but by the nature of reality"; it is a matter of "*consistency*, which, in this case, means the obligation to respect the rights of others, if one wishes one's own rights to be recognized and protected."[44] A person cannot rationally claim the protection of a principle that he repudiates in action.

We have seen the essential elements of Rand's observation-based derivation of the principle of individual rights: the truth that each individual morally must be left free to act on his own judgment, so long as he does not violate the same right of others. This principle does not come from God or from government; nor is it self-evident or "inherent" in man's nature. Rather, it is derived from observation and logic. It is discovered and formulated by looking at reality—focusing on relevant facts about the nature of values, the requirements of life, the nature of man, the propriety of egoism, the value of reason, man's need to act on his judgment, and the antilife nature of physical force—all the while integrating one's observations into concepts, generalizations, and moral principles. This is what Rand did. And this is why her theory is true.

Importantly, Rand's theory does not (as some people mistakenly believe) fall into the category of "natural rights" theory. Hers is a different theory altogether. First, whereas natural rights theory holds that rights are moral laws emanating from "super-nature" (i.e., "God"), Rand showed that rights are moral principles derived from *actual* nature. On that count, if "natural rights" theory did not have a long history of actually being God-given rights theory, it might have been appropriate to categorize Rand's theory as one of natural rights. But natural rights theory *does* have that problematic history; thus it is improper to include Rand's theory in that category.[45]

Second, "natural rights" theory holds that rights are "inherent" in man's nature—meaning, "inborn" and a part of man by virtue of the fact that he is man. But rights are not inherent or inborn[46]—which is why (a) there is no evidence to suggest that they are, and (b) belief that they are is mocked as "one with belief in witches and unicorns."

Rand's theory holds *not* that rights are "inherent," but that they are *objective*—not that they are "inborn," but that they are conceptual identifications of the factual requirements of human life in a social context. Her theory is, as this essay has endeavored to show, demonstrably true.

Unfortunately, although Rand's theory is demonstrably true, and although it solves the problems that are inherent in the traditional theories, few people today are willing to recognize and embrace it. Because our culture is steeped in the notion that self-interest is evil—and because Rand's theory is based on the fact that self-interest is *good*—many people, even upon reading or hearing Rand's argument, will ignore or deny it and continue clinging to the old saw that rights come from "God" or are somehow "inherent" in human nature. But ignoring or denying Rand's proof cannot change the fact that *real* rights—*defensible* rights—hierarchically depend on and are indeed logical extensions of egoism.

Whereas the principle of egoism is the recognition of the fact that each person should act to promote his life and is the proper beneficiary of his own life-serving actions, the principle of rights is the recognition of the fact that in order for a person to uphold the principle of egoism, he must be *free* to act on his judgment. The former principle gives rise to the latter.

Just as the concept of life makes the concept of value both possible and necessary, so too the principle of egoism makes the principle of rights both possible and necessary. And just as to speak of value as apart from life is worse than a contradiction in terms, so to speak of rights as apart from egoism is worse than a contradiction in terms—and for the same reason. "Rights" torn from their foundation in egoism are not rights but stolen concepts—concepts lifted from the foundation that gives rise to them, the foundation that connects them to reality, the foundation on which they hierarchically depend and in which they have objective meaning.

People are free to use words as they wish, but they are not free to wish away facts. Apart from egoism, rights simply have no foundation in reality.

We who want to defend man's rights to life, liberty, property, and the pursuit of happiness—we who want to live fully as human beings—must embrace and advocate the underlying ideas that support and give rise to the principle of rights. We must embrace and advocate Rand's demonstrably true theory of rights.

10

Individualism vs. Collectivism: Our Future, Our Choice

The fundamental political conflict in America today is, as it has been for a century, individualism vs. collectivism. Does the individual's life belong to him—or does it belong to the group, the community, society, or the state? With government expanding ever more rapidly—seizing and spending more and more of our money on "entitlement" programs and corporate bailouts, and intruding on our businesses and lives in increasingly onerous ways—the need for clarity on this issue has never been greater. Let us begin by defining the terms at hand.

Individualism is the idea that the individual's life belongs to him and that he has an inalienable right to live it as he sees fit, to act on his own judgment, to keep and use the product of his effort, and to pursue the values of his choosing. It's the idea that the individual is sovereign, an end in himself, and the fundamental unit of moral concern. This is the ideal that the American Founders set forth and sought to establish when they drafted the Declaration and the Constitution and created a country in which the individual's rights to life, liberty, property, and the pursuit of happiness were to be recognized and protected.

Collectivism is the idea that the individual's life belongs not to him but to the group or society of which he is merely a part, that he has no rights, and that he must sacrifice his values and goals for the group's "greater good." According to collectivism, the group or society is the basic unit of moral concern, and the individual is of value only insofar as he serves the group. As one advocate of this idea puts it: "Man has no rights except those which society permits him to enjoy. From the day of his birth until the day of his death society allows him to enjoy certain so-called rights and deprives him of others; not . . . because society desires especially to favor or oppress the individual, but because its own preservation, welfare, and happiness are the prime considerations."[1]

Individualism or collectivism—which of these ideas is correct? Which has the facts on its side?

Individualism does, and we can see this at every level of philosophic inquiry: from metaphysics, the branch of philosophy concerned with the fundamental nature of reality; to epistemology, the branch concerned with the nature and means of knowledge; to ethics, the branch concerned with the nature of value and proper human action; to politics, the branch concerned with a proper social system.

We'll take them in turn.

Metaphysics, Individualism, and Collectivism

When we look out at the world and see people, we see separate, distinct individuals. The individuals may be in groups (say, on a soccer team or in a business venture), but the indivisible beings we see are individual people. Each has his own body, his own mind, his own life. Groups, insofar as they exist, are nothing more than individuals who have come together to interact for some purpose. This is an observable fact about the way the world is. It is not a matter of personal opinion or social convention, and it is not rationally debatable. It is a perceptual-level, metaphysically given fact. Things are what they are; human beings are individuals.

A beautiful statement of the metaphysical fact of individualism was provided by former slave Frederick Douglass in a letter he wrote to his ex-"master" Thomas Auld after escaping bondage in Maryland and fleeing to New York. "I have often thought I should like to explain to you the grounds upon which I have justified myself in running away from you," wrote Douglass. "I am almost ashamed to do so now, for by this time you may have discovered them yourself. I will, however, glance at them." You see, said Douglass,

> I am myself; you are yourself; we are two distinct persons, equal persons. What you are, I am. You are a man, and so am I. God created both, and made us separate beings. I am not by nature bound to you, or you to me. Nature does not make your existence depend upon me, or mine to depend upon yours. I cannot walk upon your legs, or you upon mine. I cannot breathe for you, or you for me; I must breathe for myself, and you for yourself. We are distinct persons, and are each equally provided with faculties necessary to our individual existence. In leaving you, I took nothing but what belonged to me, and in no way lessened your means for obtaining an *honest* living. Your faculties remained yours, and mine became useful to their rightful owner.[2]

Although one could quibble with the notion that "God" creates people, Douglass's basic metaphysical point is clearly sound. Human beings are by nature distinct, separate beings, each with his own body and his own faculties necessary to his own existence. Human beings are not in any way metaphysically attached or dependent on one another; each must use his own mind and direct his own body; no one else can do either for him. People are *individuals*. "I am myself; you are yourself; we are two distinct persons."

The individual is metaphysically real; he exists in and of himself; he is the basic unit of human life. Groups or collectives of people—whether families, partnerships, communities, or societies—are not metaphysically real; they do not exist in and of themselves; they are not fundamental units of human life. Rather, they are some number of individuals. This is perceptually self-evident. We can *see* that it is true.

Who says otherwise? Collectivists do. John Dewey, a father of pragmatism and modern "liberalism," explains the collectivist notion as follows:

> Society in its unified and structural character is the fact of the case; the non-social individual is an abstraction arrived at by imagining what man would be if all his human qualities were taken away. Society, as a real whole, is the normal order, and the mass as an aggregate of isolated units is the fiction.[3]

According to collectivism, the group or society *is* metaphysically real—and the individual is a mere abstraction, a fiction.[4]

This, of course, is ridiculous, but there you have it. On the metaphysics of collectivism, you and I (and Mr. Douglass) are fictional, and we become real only insofar as we somehow interrelate with society. As to exactly *how* we must interrelate with the collective in order to become part of the "real whole," we'll hear about that shortly.

Let us turn now to the branch of philosophy concerned with the nature of knowledge.

Epistemology, Individualism, and Collectivism

What is knowledge? Where does it come from? How do we know what's true? Knowledge is a mental grasp of a fact (or facts) of reality reached by perceptual observation or a process of reason based thereon.[5] Who looks at reality, hears reality, touches reality, reasons about reality—and thereby gains knowledge of reality? The individual does. The individual possesses eyes, ears, hands, and the like. The individual possesses a mind and the capacity to use it. He perceives reality (e.g., dogs, cats, and birds, and death); he integrates his perceptions into concepts (e.g., "dog," "animal," and "mortal"); he integrates his concepts into generalizations (e.g., "dogs can bite" and "animals are mortal"); he forms principles (e.g., "animals, including man, must take certain actions in order to remain alive," and "man requires freedom in order to live and prosper"). And so on. Knowledge is a product of the perceptual observations and mental integrations of *individuals*.

Of course, individuals can learn from other people, they can teach others what they have learned—and they can do so in groups. But in any such transmission of knowledge, the individual's senses must do the perceiving, and his mind must do the integrating. Groups don't have sensory apparatuses or minds; only individuals do. This, too, is simply unassailable.

But that doesn't stop collectivists from denying it.

The relevant epistemological principle, writes Helen Longino (chair of the philosophy department at Stanford University) is that "knowledge is produced by cognitive processes that are fundamentally social." Granted, she says, "without individuals there would be no knowledge" because "it is through their sensory system that the natural world enters cognition. . . . The activities of knowledge construction, however, are the activities of individuals in interaction"; thus knowledge "is constructed not by individuals, but by an interactive dialogic community."[6]

You can't make this stuff up. But an "interactive dialogic community" can.

Although it is true (and should be unremarkable) that individuals in a society can exchange ideas and learn from one another, the fact remains that the individual, not the community, has a mind; the individual, not the group, does the thinking; the individual, not society, produces knowledge; and the individual, not society, shares that knowledge with others who, in turn, must use their individual minds if they are to grasp it. Any individual who chooses to observe the facts of reality can see that this is so. The fact that certain "philosophers" (or "dialogic communities") deny it has no bearing on the truth of the matter.

Correct epistemology—the truth about the nature and source of knowledge—is on the side of individualism, not collectivism.

Next up are the respective views of morality that follow from these foundations.

Ethics, Individualism, and Collectivism

What is the nature of good and bad, right and wrong? How, in principle, should people act? Such are the questions of ethics or morality (I use these terms interchangeably). Why do these questions arise? Why do we need to answer them? Such questions arise and need to be answered only because *individuals* exist and need principled guidance about how to live and prosper.

We are not born knowing how to survive and achieve happiness, nor do we gain such knowledge automatically, nor, if we do gain it, do we act on such knowledge automatically. (As evidence, observe the countless miserable people in the world.) If we want to live and prosper, we need principled guidance toward that end. Ethics is the branch of philosophy dedicated to providing such guidance.

For instance, a proper morality says to the individual: *Go by reason* (as against faith or feelings)—look at reality, identify the nature of things, make causal connections, use logic—because reason is your only means of knowledge, and thus your only means of choosing and achieving life-serving goals and values. Morality also says: *Be honest*—don't pretend that facts are other than they are, don't make up alternate realities in your mind and treat them as real—because reality is absolute and cannot be faked out of existence, and because you need to understand the real world in order to succeed in it. Morality further provides guidance for dealing specifically with people. For instance, it says: *Be just*—judge people rationally, according to the available and relevant facts, and treat them accordingly, as they deserve to be treated—because this policy is crucial to establishing and maintaining good relationships and to avoiding, ending, or managing bad ones. And morality says: *Be independent*—think and judge for yourself, don't turn to others for what to believe or accept—because truth is not correspondence to the views of other people but correspondence to the facts of reality. And so on.

By means of such guidance (and the foregoing is just a brief indication), morality enables the individual to live and thrive. And that is precisely the *purpose* of moral guidance: to help the individual choose and achieve life-serving goals and values, such as an education, a career, recreational activities, friendships, and romance. The purpose of morality is, as the great individualist Ayn Rand put it, to teach you to enjoy yourself and live.

Just as the individual, not the group, is metaphysically real—and just as the individual, not the collective, has a mind and thinks—so too the individual, not the community or society, is the fundamental unit of moral concern. The individual is morally an end in himself, not a means to the ends of others. Each individual should pursue his life-serving values and respect the rights of others to do the same. This is the morality that flows from the metaphysics and epistemology of individualism.

What morality flows from the metaphysics and epistemology of collectivism? Just what you would expect: a morality in which the collective is the basic unit of moral concern.

On the collectivist view of morality, explains "progressive" intellectual A. Maurice Low, "that which more than anything marks the distinction between civilized and uncivilized society is that in the former the individual is nothing and society is everything; in the latter society is nothing and the individual is everything." Mr. Low assisted with the definition of collectivism at the outset of this article; here he elaborates with emphasis on the alleged "civility" of collectivism:

> In a civilized society man has no rights except those which society permits him to enjoy. From the day of his birth until the day of his death society allows him to enjoy certain so-called rights and deprives him of others; not . . . because society desires especially to favor or oppress the individual, but because its own preservation, welfare, and happiness are the prime considerations. And so that society may not perish, so that it may reach a still higher plane, so that men and women may become better citizens, society permits them certain privileges and restricts them in the use of others. Sometimes in the exercise of this power the individual is put to a great deal of inconvenience, even, at times, he suffers what appears to be injustice. This is to be regretted, but it is inevitable. The aim of civilized society is to do the greatest good to the greatest number, and because the largest number may derive benefit from the largest good the individual must subordinate his own desires or inclinations for the benefit of all.[7]

Because Mr. Low wrote that in 1913—before Stalin, Mao, Hitler, Mussolini, Pol Pot, and company tortured and murdered hundreds of millions of people explicitly in the name of "the greatest good for the greatest number"—he may be granted some small degree of leniency. Today's collectivists, however, have no such excuse.

As Ayn Rand wrote in 1946, and as every adult who chooses to think can now appreciate,

> "The greatest good for the greatest number" is one of the most vicious slogans ever foisted on humanity. This slogan has no concrete, specific meaning. There is no way to interpret it benevolently, but a great many ways in which it can be used to justify the most vicious actions.
>
> What is the definition of "the good" in this slogan? None, except: whatever is good for the greatest number. Who, in any particular issue, decides what is good for the greatest number? Why, the greatest number.
>
> If you consider this moral, you would have to approve of the following examples, which are exact applications of this slogan in practice: fifty-one percent of humanity enslaving the other forty-nine; nine hungry cannibals eating the tenth one; a lynching mob murdering a man whom they consider dangerous to the community.
>
> There were seventy million Germans in Germany and six hundred thousand Jews. The greatest number (the Germans) supported the Nazi government which told them that their greatest good would be served by exterminating the smaller number (the Jews) and grabbing their property. This was the horror achieved in practice by a vicious slogan accepted in theory.
>
> But, you might say, the majority in all these examples did not achieve any real good for itself either? No. It didn't. Because "the good" is not determined by counting numbers and is not achieved by the sacrifice of anyone to anyone.[8]

The collectivist notion of morality is patently evil and demonstrably false. The good of the community logically cannot take priority over that of the individual because the only reason moral concepts such as "good" and "should" are necessary in the first place is that individuals exist and need principled guidance in order to sustain and further their lives. Any attempt to turn the purpose of morality against the individual—the fundamental unit of human reality and thus of moral concern—is not merely a moral crime; it is an attempt to annihilate morality as such.

To be sure, societies—consisting as they do of individuals—need moral principles, too, but *only* for the purpose of enabling individuals to act in ways necessary to sustain and further their own lives. Thus, the *one* moral principle that a society must embrace if it is to be a *civilized* society is the principle of individual rights: the recognition of the fact that each individual is morally an end in himself and has a moral prerogative to act on his judgment for his own sake, free from coercion by others. On this principle, each individual has a right to think and act as he sees fit; he has a right to produce and trade the products of his efforts voluntarily, by mutual consent to mutual benefit; he has a right to disregard complaints that he is not serving some so-called "greater good"—and no one, including groups and governments, has a moral right to force him to act against his judgment. Ever.

This brings us to the realm of politics.

Politics, Individualism, and Collectivism

The politics of individualism is essentially what the American Founders had in mind when they created the United States but were unable to implement perfectly: a land of liberty, a society in which the government does only one thing and does it well—protects the rights of all individuals equally by banning the use of physical force from social relationships and by using force only in retaliation and only against those who initiate its use. In such a society, government uses force as necessary against thieves, extortionists, murderers, rapists, terrorists, and the like—but it leaves peaceful, rights-respecting citizens *completely* free to live their lives and pursue their happiness in accordance with their own judgment.

Toward that end, a proper, rights-respecting government consists of legislatures, courts, police, a military, and any other branches and departments necessary to the protection of individual rights. This is the essence of the politics of individualism, which follows logically from the metaphysics, epistemology, and ethics of individualism.

What politics follows from those of collectivism?

"America works best when its citizens put aside individual self-interest to do great things together—when we elevate the *common good*," writes David Callahan of the collectivist think tank Demos.[9] Michael Tomasky, editor of *Democracy*, elaborates, explaining that modern "liberalism was built around the idea—the philosophical principle—that citizens should be called upon to look beyond their own self-interest and work for a greater common interest."

> This, historically, is the moral basis of liberal governance—not justice, not equality, not rights, not diversity, not government, and not even prosperity or opportunity. Liberal governance is about demanding of citizens that they balance self-interest with common interest. . . . This is the only justification leaders can make to citizens for liberal governance, really: That all are being asked to contribute to a project larger than themselves. . . . citizens sacrificing for and participating in the creation of a common good.[10]

This is the ideology of today's left in general, including, of course, President Barack Obama. As Obama puts it, we must heed the "call to sacrifice" and uphold our "core ethical and moral obligation" to "look out for one another" and to "be unified in service to a greater good."[11] "Individual actions, individual dreams, are not sufficient. We must unite in collective action, build collective institutions and organizations."[12]

But modern "liberals" and new "progressives" are not alone in their advocacy of the politics of collectivism. Joining them are impostors of the right, such as Rick Santorum, who pose as advocates of liberty but, in their perverted advocacy, annihilate the very concept of liberty.

"Properly defined," writes Santorum, "*liberty* is freedom coupled with responsibility to something bigger or higher than the self. It is the pursuit of our dreams with an eye toward the common good. Liberty is the dual activity of lifting our eyes to the heavens while at the same time extending our hands and hearts to our neighbor."[13] It is not "the freedom to be as selfish as I want to be," or "the freedom to be left alone," but "the freedom to attend to one's duties—duties to God, to family, and to neighbors."[14]

Such is the state of politics in America today, and this is the choice we face: Americans can either continue to ignore the fact that collectivism is utterly corrupt from the ground up, and thus continue down the road to statism and tyranny—or we can look at reality, use our minds, acknowledge the absurdities of collectivism and the atrocities that follow from it, and shout the truth from the rooftops and across the Internet.

What would happen if we did the latter? As Ayn Rand said, "You would be surprised how quickly the ideologists of collectivism retreat when they encounter a confident, *intellectual* adversary. Their case rests on appealing to human confusion, ignorance, dishonesty, cowardice, despair. Take the side they dare not approach; appeal to human intelligence."[15]

11

Capitalism and the Moral High Ground

Economists from Adam Smith to Ludwig von Mises to Henry Hazlitt to Thomas Sowell have elucidated the general mechanics of a free market and demonstrated the unassailable practicality of capitalism. They have shown how freer markets provide better and cheaper health care, cleaner air and water, safer automobiles and airplanes, ample food and energy, better and cheaper schools, and so on. But their arguments have not convinced the world to embrace capitalism. On the contrary, people today are condemning the system of private property as loudly as ever.

According to Congressman Jim Moran (D-VA), Americans must abandon "this simplistic notion that people who have wealth are entitled to keep it."[1] Congresswoman Maxine Waters (D-CA), addressing oil company CEOs, openly threatens to socialize their industry: "Guess what this liberal would be all about. This liberal will be about socializing. . . . all of your companies."[2] Philosopher Noam Chomsky insists that "putting people in charge of their own assets breaks down the solidarity that comes from doing something together, and diminishes the sense that people have responsibility for each other."[3]

All such assaults on free markets and property rights proceed from the recognition of the fact that these key elements of capitalism enable *selfishness*. As Karl Marx explained: "The right of man to property is the right to enjoy his possessions and dispose of the same arbitrarily, without regard for other men, independently from society, the right of selfishness."[4] And as President-elect Barack Obama intimates, who would dare "to make a virtue out of selfishness"?[5]

How do so-called advocates of capitalism respond to accusations of its inherent selfishness? Some, such as George Gilder, simply deny it. Selfishness is not the essence of capitalism, writes Gilder, "Altruism is the essence of capitalism. . . . Capitalism begins with giving. . . . The deepest truths of capitalism are faith, hope, and love."[6] This, of course, is ridiculous. Capitalism begins not with giving but with producing—and then moves on to keeping, using, and trading the product of one's efforts for other values in the marketplace. Nor is capitalism based on faith or hope; rather, it is based on reason and long-term planning, which are the means by which businessmen succeed and grow rich. And although love is certainly essential to capitalism, the relevant object of love in this context is money. Capitalism is the system of the selfish pursuit of profit, and to deny this, as Gilder does, is to abuse the meaning of words.

Other "defenders" of capitalism, such as Michael Novak, attempt to reconcile its selfish nature with conventional morality:

> While recognizing that no system of political economy can escape the ravages of human sinfulness, [capitalism] has attempted to set in place a system which renders sinful tendencies as productive of good as possible. While basing itself on something less than perfect virtue,

> reasoned self-interest, it has attempted to draw from self-interest its most creative potential. It is a system designed for sinners, in the hope of achieving as much moral good as individuals and communities can generate under conditions of ample liberty.[7]

So, by freeing sinners to pursue their reasoned self-interest, capitalism taps into the creative potential of these depraved souls and thereby achieves moral good. This, too, is absurd. To concede the immorality of a social system is to concede the argument for it. The attempt to defend capitalism on the grounds that it is morally bad (or, at best, neutral) but economically good is precisely what has failed the aforementioned economists.

The practicality of capitalism is insufficient grounds for its defense against those who assert its immorality. We who wish to advocate capitalism must do so on *moral* grounds. The moral grounds on which we must advocate capitalism, however, are not those of conventional wisdom.

Capitalism enables everyone to act in a consistently self-interested manner. Rather than shying away from this unassailable fact, we must embrace and emphasize it. We must do so not on the pragmatic grounds that doing so will work to defend capitalism (which it will), but on the principled grounds that the selfishness-enabling characteristic of capitalism is, in fact, what makes it the only moral social system on earth.

To see why this is so, let us begin by observing how capitalism enables economic selfishness and what this means in practice.

Under genuine capitalism—not the mongrel system operative in America today, but pure, unregulated, *laissez-faire* capitalism—the government prohibits citizens from using physical force against each other, and the Constitution prohibits the government from using force against citizens except in retaliation against those who initiate its use. Thus everyone is fully free to act on his own judgment for his own sake.

Consider the activities of a bank under capitalism. If an individual or corporation chooses to create a bank, he or it is free to establish the policy that the bank will offer loans only to individuals and businesses the bank regards as creditworthy. The government may not force the bank to lend money to those it regards as unable to repay a loan or as too risky for business. Nor may the government dictate or limit the interest rates or other terms or conditions that the bank chooses to offer. The government may not force the bank to do anything, because under capitalism, the government is forbidden to initiate force against citizens or businesses.

The bank owner or owners are free to decide how they will run their business at every step and turn; free to open new branches, to purchase other banks, to purchase insurance companies, and to expand or diversify their bank in countless other ways. They are free to maximize their profits and to grow and thrive and prosper to the best of their ability. The only thing they are not free to do is to use physical force or fraud (indirect force) against people, because, under capitalism, physical force is banned from social relationships.[8]

If the bank employs rational policies and succeeds, its success is good for the bank, good for its owners, and good for its customers. If the bank engages in irrational policies—if, for instance, its risk-assessment procedures are such that it regularly lends money to people who cannot repay their loans—the bank suffers negative financial consequences. If its policies lead the bank to failure, it may not seek a bailout from the government; nor may the government offer to "rescue" the bank. Under capitalism, bankers and banks, like all individuals and businesses, are responsible for the consequences of their decisions, whether good or bad, profitable or not. Consequently, under capitalism, if a bank fails, it files bankruptcy or offers itself for sale on the cheap or goes out of business; its owners suffer losses; and its customers find other means through which to save or borrow money. Under capitalism, everyone is free to benefit from his rational choices and actions, and no one may force others to suffer the consequences of his irrational decisions.

Capitalism encourages rationality in the marketplace. Those who act in a rationally self-interested manner tend to succeed, and those who do succeed are free to enjoy the fruits of their rationality.

Consider the case of an automaker. Under capitalism, an automaker is free to manufacture and market cars in whatever way it sees fit, and the company is free to succeed or to fail accordingly. The government may not force the company to sell a particular kind of car, nor force it to pay its employees a particular minimum or maximum wage, nor force it to contract with a particular vendor, nor a union, nor anyone else. The automaker is free to make all such decisions according to its own judgment (i.e., the judgment of its owners). If the automaker uses good judgment and succeeds, it is free to keep, use, and dispose of its profits. If it uses poor judgment and fails—or if its competitors outperform it such that it cannot remain profitable—the automaker may file for bankruptcy or offer itself for sale or close its doors. But it may not seek a bailout from the government. Under capitalism, individuals and corporations legally own not only their profits but also their problems, and the government is prohibited from intervening in the marketplace.

As to unions, under capitalism, individuals are free to band together and to stipulate that members of their group will work only on certain terms and under certain conditions. But such groups may not force others to contract with them, nor may the government employ such force on their behalf. Under capitalism, everyone is free to set his own terms and conditions of contract; no one may infringe on the freedom of others to set theirs; everyone is equally free to be fully selfish.

Capitalism is the system of mutual self-interest and mutual non-interference. Everyone who wishes to live well and prosper is free to do so to the best of his effort and ability; no one may stop another from pursuing his values or goals.

Consider a real-estate development company. Under capitalism, the company is free to build condominiums or pharmaceutical plants or whatever else it wants to build, and its owners are free to use and dispose of their profits according to their own judgment. But if the company needs to acquire real estate on which to build, it may acquire that property only from willing sellers. If, by mutual consent to mutual advantage, it can acquire the property from those who own it, the company is free to develop that property. If, however, the owners of the property in question do not want to sell it to the development company, the company may not force them to "sell"—nor may it enlist the government to do so. The company may increase its offer or change its plans or proceed peacefully in another manner, but it may not resort to coercion because, under capitalism, coercion is forbidden.

Capitalism is the system of private property and voluntary exchange. Those who are willing to interact peacefully with others are free to produce, trade, and prosper accordingly. Those who wish to use force against their fellow men are precluded from doing so—and punished if they try.

Under capitalism, the initiation of physical force is barred from human relationships; citizens delegate the use of retaliatory force to the government, which may use force only in retaliation and only against those who initiate its use; and those who initiate force against others are met with force by the law.[9] This arrangement leaves everyone free to act on his own judgment for his own sake as a matter of principle. This is what makes capitalism the system of selfishness—and this is what distinguishes capitalism from all other social systems.

Consider the alternative systems in this regard. Under *communism*, the government forces individuals and businesses to act against their judgment for the sake of the "workers" or the "community"; hence the term "communism" (e.g., the USSR). Under *socialism*, the government forces individuals and businesses to act against their judgment for the sake of the "collective" or "society"; hence the term "socialism" (e.g., present-day Sweden). Under *theocracy*, the government forces individuals and businesses to act against their judgment in obedience to "God's will"—or whatever His earthly "representatives" deem His will to be; hence the term "theocracy," which means literally "rule by God" (e.g., present-day Iran). Under *fascism*, the government forces individuals and businesses to act against their judgment for the sake of the "nation," the "race," the "people," the "elderly," the "poor," or some other "group"; hence the term "fascism," which means literally "group-ism" (e.g., Mussolini's Italy).

Under capitalism (which has yet to exist),[10] the government is forbidden from forcing individuals or businesses to act against their judgment. In a capitalist society, everyone is legally free to act on his own judgment for his own sake. The government serves only to protect individuals and businesses from physical force by banning it from social relationships and by using retaliatory force as necessary against those who initiate its use.

America today is a motley mixture of all of the above. Our federal, state, and local governments force citizens to act against their judgment in myriad ways: for the sake of the community (e.g., the Community Reinvestment Act, which forces banks to lend money to unqualified borrowers); for the sake of the workers (e.g., the United Auto Workers union, whose demands the government forces on automakers and other businesses); for the sake of society (e.g., Social Security, through which the government forces some citizens to fund the retirement of others); for the sake of "God" (e.g., faith-based initiatives, through which the government forces Americans to fund "God's" earthly agents); for the sake of the nation (e.g., the Federal Trade Commission, through which the government forces businesses not to be too successful because too much business success allegedly would harm consumers); for the sake of race (e.g., affirmative action laws, through which the government forces businesses and schools to hire or admit people on the basis of genetic lineage); for the sake of the people (e.g., eminent domain laws, through which the government forces property owners to relinquish their homes, businesses, and land for so-called public purposes); for the sake of the elderly (e.g., Medicare, through which the government forces younger Americans to fund the health care of older Americans); for the sake of the poor (e.g., Medicaid, through which the government forces working Americans to fund the health care of allegedly destitute Americans); and for the sake of the group in general (e.g., the Food and Drug Administration, through which the government forces doctors, patients, drugmakers, food producers, and consumers to act against their judgment on the grounds that the group's judgment, as represented by the "experts" at the FDA, is better for everyone). Granted, this list barely scratches the surface, but it indicates the enormity of government coercion against Americans today.

Despite all this force, however, Americans are, in some respects, still free to act on their judgment for their own sake: free to choose their careers, their hobbies, and their residences—providing that their choices do not "harm" the "environment"; free to marry their lovers—unless their lovers happen to share their gender; free to have an abortion—unless doing so would involve intact dilation and extraction; free to speak their minds—except with respect to certain kinds of political speech, broadcasting, and advertising; free to keep, use, and dispose of their earnings—except the large percentage taken by federal, state, and local governments via taxation; and free to offer employment to whomever they choose—except would-be immigrants from countries that have reached their quotas for emigration to the land of waning liberty.

In short, Americans are partially forced to act against their judgment and partially free to act in accordance with their judgment.

What is the moral status of this arrangement? The arrangement is immoral—immoral because, insofar as the government forces people to act against their judgment, it impedes their ability to live fully as human beings.

Man lives by acting on his rational judgment. In order to survive and prosper, he must observe reality, integrate his observations into concepts, identify causal relationships, form principles about the kind of actions that are good and bad for his life, and act on his best judgment. This is true in every area of human life and observable at every stage of human history.

Man's rational judgment is the means by which he learned to make tools for hunting and fishing, to lash together branches and build shelters, to make and control fire, and to shape and bake bricks. It is the means by which he grasped the nature of plants and soil, developed irrigation systems, discovered the principles of agriculture, and proceeded to mass-produce food. It is the means by which he discovered the chemical elements of the earth, the principles of chemistry, and how to produce plastics, medicines, energy, and countless other life-serving values based on that knowledge. It is the means by which he learned about wings and flight, discovered the principles of aerodynamics, and proceeded to build and fly jumbo jets. It is the means by which he discovered the need for money and credit, the principles of banking, and how to evaluate borrowers and assess risk. It is the means by which he learned how to manufacture and market automobiles, how to manage employees, and how to assess their worth in the context of a corporation. And it is the means by which he discovered the need of private property, voluntary trade, and a government that protects each individual's right to life, liberty, property, and the pursuit of happiness.

Reason is man's basic means of living, and reason is an attribute of the *individual*. Although individuals can work together in groups—and can do so to great benefit—the fact remains that only individuals can think, because only individuals have minds. Excepting the mentally retarded, each individual's own mind is his own basic means of living, and each individual is faced with the alternative of choosing to use his mind or not. If he chooses to think, he can live and prosper. If he chooses not to think, he either dies or survives parasitically on the efforts of those who do choose to think. Either way, reason is man's basic means of living, and if an individual is to live as a human being, rather than as a parasite, he must think rationally and act accordingly.[11]

So the crucial question in the realm of politics is: What can stop an individual from acting on his rational judgment? There is only one thing that can stop an individual from acting on his judgment: other people. And there is only one means by which they can do it: physical force. Physical force used against a person stops him from employing his basic means of living: the judgment of his mind.

If a man judges that he should build a house, he is free to do so—unless another person, group, or government forcibly stops him from doing so. If a woman judges that she should start a business in her home, she is free to do so—unless another person, group, or government forcibly stops her from doing so. If a banker judges that he should withhold loans from those with insufficient income or poor credit, or if an automaker judges that he should refrain from hiring employees at rates that will drive him out of business, or if an individual judges that he should accept employment at an entry-level rate offered by an employer, or if a property owner judges that he should retain his property, the individuals or owners in question are free to act on their own judgment—unless a person, group, or government forcibly stops them from doing so.

Because an individual's judgment is his basic means of living, physical force, to the extent that it is used against him, causes him to lead a less than human life. This fact gives rise to man's need of a principle that precludes people, groups, and governments from using force against individuals. That principle is the principle of individual rights.

The principle of individual rights is the recognition of the fact that in order to live fully as a human being, an individual must be fully free to act on his own judgment for his own sake.[12] If recognized and upheld, however, this principle would enable everyone to act consistently selfishly as a matter of principle—and this possibility runs counter to conventional morality.

This brings us to the crux of the battle for capitalism.

If human beings are to *act* on their rational judgment, they must be *free* to act on it. Capitalism is the social system that recognizes this fact and upholds the principle of individual rights. But according to the dominant morality today, altruism, the individual does not and cannot have a right to act on his own judgment for his own sake, because the individual has a "duty" to sacrifice his judgment and thus his life for the sake of others.

Altruism holds that being moral consists not in being selfish but in being self*less*, not in self-interestedly pursuing and protecting one's life-serving values but in self-sacrificially serving others. ("Alter" is Latin for "other"; "altruism" means "other-ism.") And because pushers of altruism frequently equivocate on the meaning of the concept of "service," it is crucial for advocates of capitalism to grasp the actual meaning of this concept as it relates to altruism.

Altruism does not call merely for "serving" others; it calls for *self-sacrificially* serving others. Otherwise, Michael Dell would have to be considered more altruistic than Mother Teresa. Why? Because Michael Dell serves millions more people than Mother Teresa ever did. The difference, of course, is in the way he serves people. Whereas Mother Teresa "served" people by exchanging her time and effort for *nothing*, Michael Dell serves people by *trading* with them—by exchanging value for value to mutual advantage—an exchange in which both sides *gain*.

Trading value for value is not the same thing as *giving up* values for nothing. There is a black-and-white difference between pursuing values and giving them up, between achieving values and relinquishing them, between exchanging a *lesser* value for a *greater* one and vice versa.

A sacrifice is not "any choice or action that precludes some other choice or action." A sacrifice is the surrender of a greater value for the sake of a lesser value or a non-value.[13]

For example, if a parent forgoes a game of golf with his friend in order to spend the morning preparing for his son's birthday party that afternoon, he has not committed a sacrifice. If his son's party means more to his life than does the game of golf, then the sacrifice would be to forgo the preparation and play the game.

Similarly, if a student knows that his education is more important to his life than is a night on the town with his friends, then staying home to study for a crucial exam, against the urgings of his buddies, does not constitute a sacrifice. The sacrifice would be to forgo his judgment, hit the town, and botch the exam.

Likewise, if a man wants to become a banker because he is fascinated by the profession and thinks he will love that career, and if he forgoes his second choice, a career in law, in order to create a bank, then he has not committed a sacrifice. He has pursued the greater of the two values. If however, he decides to quit banking and become a bureaucrat on the grounds that selfless "public service" is the "right thing to do," then he has committed a sacrifice. He has abandoned what he regards as his ideal career in order to selflessly serve others—and, consequently, he will lead a less happy life.

Life requires that we regularly forgo lesser values for the sake of greater ones. But these are *gains*, not sacrifices. A sacrifice consists in giving up something that is *more* important to one's life for the sake of something that is *less* important (or non-important) to one's life. A sacrifice results in a *personal loss.*

Whereas capitalism is the politics of self-interest and personal gain, altruism is the ethics of self-sacrifice and personal loss. And altruism does not countenance self-interest or personal gain. This is not a caricature of altruism; it is the *essence* of the morality. As philosophy professor Peter Singer, an arch advocate of altruism, writes: "To the extent that [people] are motivated by the prospect of obtaining a reward or avoiding a punishment, they are not acting altruistically. . . ."[14] As philosophy professor Thomas Nagel, another advocate of altruism, explains, altruism entails "a willingness to act in consideration of the interests of other persons, without the need of ulterior motives"—"ulterior motives" meaning: personal gains.[15] And as the philosopher Ayn Rand, the arch opponent of altruism, succinctly put it: "The basic principle of altruism is that man has no right to exist for his own sake, that service to others is the only justification of his existence, and that self-sacrifice is his highest moral duty, virtue and value."[16]

On the principle of altruism, a banker has no right to withhold a mortgage loan from someone on the selfish grounds that providing the loan would result in a loss; it is not moral to be "motivated by the prospect of obtaining a reward or avoiding a punishment"; it is wrong to selfishly pursue profit. He must serve others "without the need of ulterior motives"; he must *self-sacrificially* serve others—in this case, those who want to own a home.

Likewise, on the principle of altruism, an automaker has no right to pay employees an hourly rate that makes selfish sense for the business; it is wrong to establish terms and conditions with the "ulterior motive" of making money or remaining viable. The automaker must *self-sacrificially* serve others—such as union workers.

Nor on the principle of altruism does a property owner have a right to keep, use, and dispose of his belongings. If others—such as a real-estate development company whose proposed project would lead to higher tax revenues for the municipality—need the property owner's property, he has no right to withhold it for his selfish interests. According to altruism, he must "act in consideration of the interests of other persons"; he must *sacrifice* himself, his judgment, his property for the sake of others—in this case, the community-minded development company and the community it aims to "help."

Altruism, the morality that forbids people to act in a self-interested manner, is entirely incompatible with capitalism, the system that enables and encourages everyone to act in a *consistently* self-interested manner. Acceptance of the altruistic premise that being moral consists in self-sacrificially serving others is what gives rise to and supports the various forms of statism—communism, socialism, theocracy, fascism—and it is what is driving America toward tyranny today.

The good news for lovers of liberty is that altruism is *false*. There are no facts that give rise to the notion that one should self-sacrificially serve others, which is why no one has ever presented such facts. Consequently, adherence to altruism is irrational. There is *no reason* to sacrifice, which is why no one has ever given a reason. As Ayn Rand pointed out:

> There is one word—a single word—which can blast the morality of altruism out of existence and which it cannot withstand—the word: "*Why?*" *Why* must man live for the sake of others? *Why* must he be a sacrificial animal? *Why* is that the good? There is no earthly reason for it—and, ladies and gentlemen, in the whole history of philosophy no *earthly* reason has ever been given.[17]

Of course, alleged reasons have been given, but not legitimate ones. And those who wish to advocate capitalism need to understand why the alleged reasons are illegitimate. Here they are, along with the reasons why they are not reasons: (These fallacies are mentioned in chapter 4 as well. I repeat them here because understanding the baseless nature of altruism is essential to advocating and defending capitalism.)

1. *"You should sacrifice because God (or some other voice from another dimension) says so."* This is not a reason—certainly not an earthly one. At best, it is an appeal to authority—that is, to the "authorities" who claim to speak for God. Just because a preacher or a book makes a claim does not mean the claim is true. The Bible claims, among other things, that a bush spoke. More fundamentally, this non-reason is an arbitrary claim because there is no evidence for the existence of a god. But even those who believe

in a god can recognize the fallacy of appealing to an authority.

2. *"You should sacrifice because that's the general consensus."* This is not a reason but an appeal to the masses. Matters of truth and morality are not determined by consensus. That slavery should be legal used to be the general consensus in America, and is still the consensus in parts of Africa. That did not and does not make it so. Nor does consensus legitimize the notion that you or anyone else should sacrifice or be sacrificed.

3. *"You should sacrifice because other people need the benefit of your sacrifice."* This is an appeal to pity. Even if other people did need the benefit of your sacrifice, it would not follow that this is a reason to sacrifice. More importantly, however, the notion that people need the benefit of your sacrifice is false. What people need is to produce values and to trade them with others who produce values. And to do so, they and others must be *free* to produce and trade according to their own judgment. This, not human sacrifice, is what human life requires. (I'll touch on the relationship between freedom and egoism a little later.)

4. *"You should sacrifice because if you don't, you will be beaten, or fined, or thrown in jail, or in some other way physically assaulted."* The threat of force is not a reason; it is the opposite of a reason. If the force wielders could offer a reason why you should sacrifice, then they would not have to use force; they could use persuasion instead of coercion.

5. *"You should sacrifice because, well, when you grow up or wise up you'll see that you should."* This is not a reason, but a personal attack and an insult. It says, in effect, "If you don't see the virtue of sacrifice, then you're childish or stupid"—as if demanding a reason in support of a moral conviction could indicate a lack of maturity or intelligence.

6. *"You should sacrifice because only a miscreant or a scoundrel would challenge this established fact."* This kind of claim

assumes that you regard others' opinions of you as more important than your own judgment of truth. It is also an example of what Ayn Rand called "The Argument from Intimidation": the attempt to substitute psychological pressure for rational argument. Like the personal attack, it is an attempt to avoid having to present a rational case for a position for which no rational case can be made.

Such are the "reasons" offered in support of the claim that you should sacrifice. Far from being reasons, each is a textbook logical fallacy.

There is no reason to sacrifice—but there *is* a reason to act in a self-interested manner: your life and happiness depend on it. And there is a reason to advocate a social system that enables you and everyone else to act in a self-interested manner: your life and happiness—and the lives and happiness of all your loved ones—depend on it. Reasons do not get any better than these.

Advocates of capitalism must come to see that self-sacrifice is not moral but evil—evil because it is irrational and anti-life. Man's life does not require that he give up the values on which his life depends. It requires the opposite. It requires that he pursue and protect his life-serving values. And it requires a social system that enables him to do so. Human life requires capitalism: the social system of universal selfishness and prosperity. And if we are to defend capitalism, we must repudiate the morality of self-sacrifice and embrace the morality of self-interest: rational egoism.

Rational egoism calls not for self-sacrifice but for rational self-interest (the only kind of self-interest there is). It calls for everyone to pursue his life-serving values while respecting the rights of others to do the same.

Egoism does not call for "doing whatever one pleases" or

"doing whatever one feels like doing" or "stabbing others in the back to get what one wants." Those are caricatures of egoism perpetrated by pushers of altruism who seek to equate egoism with hedonism and subjectivism. Egoism does not hold pleasure or feelings as the standard of value. It holds *man's life* as the standard of value—and *reason* as man's basic means of living.[20]

According to rational egoism, that which promotes man's life is good, and that which harms or destroys man's life is evil. There are several highly developed principles involved in this morality—including the supreme value of reason; the crucial need of purposeful goals and self-esteem; and the virtues of productiveness, independence, honesty, integrity, justice, and pride.[21] But the key *political* principle of rational egoism is the principle of individual rights.

Whereas egoism identifies the fact that people must think rationally and act accordingly in order to live and prosper, the principle of individual rights identifies the fact that if people are to act in accordance with their judgment, they must be *free* to do so. Whereas altruism underlies and supports statism, egoism underlies and supports capitalism.

As the politics of self-interest, capitalism cannot be defended with the ethics of self-sacrifice—nor can it be defended apart from a moral foundation (e.g., via libertarianism or mere economics). We who wish to advocate capitalism must advocate it explicitly on moral grounds. We must unabashedly explain to our allies and potential allies (i.e., people who are willing to think) that human life requires rationally self-interested action; that each individual has a moral right to act on his own judgment for his own sake, so long as he does not violate the same rights of others; that capitalism is moral because it enables everyone to act in a rationally self-interested manner; and that a mixed economy—in which no one's rights are fully protected, and everyone's rights are partially violated—is immoral because it precludes people from acting fully as human life requires.

We who wish to advocate capitalism must take the moral high ground—which is ours by logical right—and we must never cede an inch to those who claim that self-sacrifice is a virtue. It is not. Self-interest is a virtue. Indeed, acting in one's rational self-interest while respecting the rights of others to do the same is the *basic* requirement of human life. And capitalism is the only social system that fully legalizes it. Grounds do not get more moral than that.

12

The Argument from Intimidation: A Confession of Intellectual Impotence

Have you heard?

- "Only a fool would deny that climate change is leading to disaster."
- "Only a xenophobe would advocate the screening of immigrants."
- "There can be no honest denial of the existence of God."
- "There can be no honest acceptance of the existence of God."
- "Only a misogynist would deny a woman's right to abortion."
- "Only a philistine could fail to see the profundity of Duchamp."
- "Only an idiot would vote for Trump."

Such assertions rarely are made so bluntly or forthrightly. More often they are insinuated ("Really? You don't get Duchamp?") or conveyed via facial expressions or other nonverbal means (a grimace, a glare, a wide-eyed stare). But you no doubt have heard such claims and encountered such expressions in one form or another. And you likely have seen people back down or change their positions in response.

Why? What's going on here?

Ayn Rand observed such behavior repeatedly, and in the *Ayn Rand Letter* she relayed two personal encounters that helped her to understand the phenomenon. The first incident, she explained,

> was a private discussion in which I was presenting my political ideas. My opponent exclaimed indignantly, in rebuttal: "I've never heard of such a thing!" "Well, you're hearing it now," I said. This had some peculiar effect on him, out of proportion to the meaning of my words; it was as if I had cut the ground from under his feet; he argued half-heartedly a little longer, then gave up.
>
> It was not till much later that I understood what it was that he had been telegraphing by the second-hander's code: "Since no one else has said such a thing before, who are you to say it?" My answer told him who I was: it rejected any second-hand sanction and demanded that he focus on the facts of reality. On such terms, he was unable to argue or to think.
>
> The second incident took place when I was working in Hollywood. A literary agent approached me with an offer from a major studio that wanted me to write a novel for one of their stars, on a theme and subject of their own choice, a novel that would be published first as a book, then made into a movie. I answered that I don't write novels to order. He said, in an oddly resentful, accusatory manner: "Many good writers are doing it." I answered

> cheerfully: "Then I guess I'm not a good writer." Again, this had some peculiar, disproportionate, ground-cutting effect on him; he argued half-heartedly a little longer, then gave up.
>
> Later, I grasped what he had been signaling between the lines. He was threatening me with the fact that *good* writers do not share my attitude. What my answer told him was: "If such are their values, then I do not care to be regarded as good by their standards." He had no further arguments to offer.[1]

In these and similar encounters, Rand saw a pattern: In each case, someone was attempting to substitute psychological pressure for rational argument. She termed this fallacy "The Argument from Intimidation."

In her article by that title (in *The Virtue of Selfishness*), Rand further observed that this fallacy "bears a certain resemblance to the fallacy *ad hominem*." Whereas ad hominem "consists of attempting to refute an argument by impeaching the character of its proponent"—for example, "Candidate X is immoral, therefore his argument is false"—the argument from intimidation

> consists of threatening to impeach an opponent's character by means of his argument, thus impeaching the argument without debate. Example: "Only the immoral can fail to see that Candidate X's argument is false."
>
> In the first case, Candidate X's immorality (real or invented) is offered as proof of the falsehood of his argument. In the second case, the falsehood of his argument is asserted arbitrarily and offered as proof of his immorality. . . .
>
> The pattern is always: "Only those who are evil (dishonest, heartless, insensitive, ignorant, etc.) can hold such an idea."[2]

If you revisit the examples at the beginning of this article, you'll see that this is exactly what's going on there. And if you set a standing order to look for instances of this fallacy, you'll detect them disturbingly often.

The fallacy is especially common in attacks on Ayn Rand, her novels, and her philosophy. Given that Rand rejected mysticism, altruism, collectivism, and statism in favor of reason, egoism, individualism, and capitalism—and given that her ideas are supported by evidence and logic—such attacks are not surprising. But they are ironic.

For instance, Paul Krugman writes that Rand's *Atlas Shrugged* "is a perennial favorite among adolescent boys. Most boys eventually outgrow it. Some, however, remain devotees for life."[3]Translation: Only those with the maturity level of an adolescent boy could find value in *Atlas Shrugged*.

Kevin Williamson writes that interest in Rand's ideas is "a kind of guilty adolescent enthusiasm . . . an intellectual mullet, a stage one goes through between the ages of 14 and 20."[4] Translation: Only the intellectually immature could appreciate Objectivism.

Heidi Moore writes, "Rand has a bit of a reputation problem among those who have not drunk the Kool-Aid."[5] Translation: Only a cultist would have anything to do with Ayn Rand.

John Gray writes, "Rand's thought has no serious intellectual content, but that has not prevented it from being taken seriously by people ignorant of the history of ideas."[6] Translation: Only those ignorant of the history of ideas could take Rand's ideas seriously.

And Sam Harris, apparently striving for gold in the Intimidation Olympics, writes:

> I often get emails from people who insist that Rand was a genius—and one who has been unfairly neglected by writers like myself. I also get emails from people who have been "washed in the blood of the Lamb," or otherwise saved by the "living Christ," who have decided to pray for my soul. It is hard for me to say which of these sentiments I find less compelling. [Translation: Rand is like a religious leader and her fans are like religionists.]
>
> As someone who has written and spoken at length about how we might develop a truly "objective" morality, I am often told by followers of Rand that their beloved guru [another instance] accomplished this task long ago. The result was Objectivism—a view that makes a religious fetish [yet another instance] of selfishness and disposes of altruism and compassion as character flaws.[7]
>
> If nothing else, this approach to ethics was a triumph of marketing, as Objectivism is basically autism rebranded.[8] [Translation: Only those with a socially and emotionally debilitating condition could find Objectivism appealing.]

People who engage in the argument from intimidation do so because, as Rand put it, "they have no arguments, no evidence, no proof, no reason, no ground to stand on." Their use of this method "is a confession of intellectual impotence."[9]

How then should people of reason deal with those who engage in such non-argument arguments? If we choose to address them at all (and there's no "duty" to do so), we should demand that they provide rational arguments in support of their claims. If they refuse, then we should name the fallacy they've committed and inform them that their confession is duly noted. This helps to keep intellectual discourse civil.

Endnotes

NB: For uniformity, the endnotes are reprinted here as they originally appeared in the articles published in *The Objective Standard.*

1. The Beauty of Ayn Rand's Ethics

1. See Ayn Rand, "Causality Versus Duty" in *Philosophy: Who Needs It* (New York: Signet, 1982), 95–101.
2. For more on the Objectivist ethics, see Ayn Rand, "The Objectivist Ethics," in *The Virtue of Selfishness* (New York: Signet, 1964), 13–39. See also Craig Biddle, *Loving Life: The Morality of Self-Interest and the Facts that Support It* (Richmond, VA: Glen Allen Press, 2002).

2. Secular, Objective Morality: Look and See

1. For example, in the Bible, God deliberately drowns practically everyone on earth (Genesis 6:7); calls for the murder of blasphemers (e.g., Leviticus 24:16), infidels (e.g., Deuteronomy 13:6–9), homosexuals (e.g., Leviticus 20:13), and children who curse or disobey their parents (e.g., Leviticus 20:9, Deuteronomy 21:18–21); and condones slavery (e.g., Leviticus 25:44, Deuteronomy 15:12) and rape (e.g., Deuteronomy 22:28–29, Numbers 31:15–18). Likewise, in the Koran, God calls for the murder of unbelievers (e.g., 2:191, 9:5) and for making sex slaves of their wives and daughters (e.g., 4:24, 33:50).
2. See Ayn Rand, "The Objectivist Ethics," in *The Virtue of Selfishness* (New York: Signet, 1964), 13.
3. Recognition of this fact is the death knell of the entire duty-based approach to ethics advocated by Immanuel Kant and his followers. If man needs morality or values, then he must need them for some life-serving purpose. What else could "need" mean? If man doesn't need values, then there is no point in telling him which values, much less which code of values, he should adopt.

4. See Rand, "The Objectivist Ethics," 16.
5. See Rand, "The Objectivist Ethics," 16.
6. Rand, "The Objectivist Ethics," 16.
7. Rand, "The Objectivist Ethics," 16.
8. See Rand, "The Objectivist Ethics," 17.
9. See Rand, "The Objectivist Ethics," 17.
10. Observe, in this connection, that people who use moral terms—such as "good" and "evil," or "should" and "shouldn't"—while denying the existence of free will commit the fallacy Ayn Rand called "concept stealing," which consists in using a concept while ignoring or denying a more fundamental concept or fact on which it logically depends. If people have no choice in their actions, if they are predetermined to act as they do, then moral terms have no referents in reality. What could "ought" mean if a person has no more choice in what he does than he did about whether or not to be born? What could "evil" mean if everything people do is as out of their control as the fact that water is wet? The existence of morality depends on the existence of free will. Thus, to use a concept such as "morality" or "virtue" or "should" or the like while denying the existence of free will is to rip the concept away from its foundation and the context that gives it meaning. For a particularly egregious example of this fallacy, see Sam Harris's denial of free will in conjunction with his book *The Moral Landscape: How Science Can Determine Human Values* (New York: Free Press, 2010). In that book, Harris sets forth his views on how we can know what is moral and immoral and how we should and shouldn't act. However, he also says that "free will is an illusion" and that "you are no more responsible for the next thing you think (and therefore *do*) than you are for the fact that you were born into this world" (104). Well, if people don't have free will and are not responsible for their thoughts or actions, why write a book about how people *should* and *shouldn't* act? If they have no choice in the matter, they have no choice in the matter.
11. See my essay "The Creed of Sacrifice vs. The Land of Liberty," *The Objective Standard*, Fall 2009.
12. See my article "Altruism: The Morality of Logical Fallacies," TOS Blog, May 22, 2006, https://www.theobjectivestandard.com/2006/05/altruism-the-morality-of-logical-fallacies/.
13. Whereas the broadest, most basic definition of the concept "value" is, "that which one acts to gain or keep," once we have used this basic definition in conjunction with various other observations and integrations to arrive at the objective standard of moral value (i.e., the requirements of human life), we can then see that a *morally correct* value is defined as, "that which one rationally acts to gain or keep for the purpose of sustaining or furthering one's life." For more on these two definitions, see Leonard Peikoff, "Unity in Epistemology and Ethics" lecture (New Milford: Second Renaissance Books, 1997); and my book *Loving Life*, especially chapters 3, 4, and 6.
14. Rand, "The Objectivist Ethics," 26.

15. The choice to use reason or not to use it—to think or not to think—is, as Rand observed, the locus of our free will. Free will "is your mind's freedom to think or not, the only will you have, your only freedom, the choice that controls all the choices you make and determines your life and your character." Rand, *For the New Intellectual* (New York: Signet, 1963), 127.
16. See Rand, "The Objectivist Ethics," 28.
17. See Rand, "The Objectivist Ethics," 29.
18. See Rand, "The Objectivist Ethics," 28.
19. *The Objective Standard*, Fall 2011.
20. For more on the nature of individualism and its opposite, collectivism, see my essay, "Individualism vs. Collectivism: Our Future, Our Choice," in *The Objective Standard*, Spring 2012.
21. See Ayn Rand, "Introducing Objectivism," in *The Voice of Reason* (New York: Meridian, 1990), 4.
22. *The Virtue of Selfishness* (New York: Signet, 1964); *Loving Life* (Richmond, VA: Glen Allen Press, 2002).

3. The Is-Altruism Dichotomy

1. See *Ancilla to the Pre-Socratic Philosophers*, trans. Kathleen Freeman (Cambridge: Harvard University Press, 1996), p. 125; and Wilhelm Windelband, *A History of Philosophy* (New York: Harper & Row, 1958), vol. I, pp. 91–94.
2. See David Hume, *Enquiries Concerning Human Understanding and Concerning the Principles of Morals* (Oxford: Clarendon Press, 1975), Appendix I, esp. pp. 287–89, 292–94; and *Treatise of Human Nature* (Oxford: Clarendon Press, 1978), Book III, esp. pp. 457–59, 462–70.
3. Sean Carroll, "The Moral Equivalent of the Parallel Postulate," *Discover*, March 24, 2010, http://blogs.discovermagazine.com/cosmicvariance/2010/03/24/the-moral-equivalent-of-the-parallel-postulate/.
4. Although some contemporary intellectuals are open to the possibility that moral principles can be derived from facts of reality, to my knowledge none (other than Ayn Rand) has shown how this can be done. In the absence of specific knowledge of how it can be done, intellectuals are effectively in the position of conceding that it can't be done. The "is-ought dichotomy" goes by other names as well, including the "fact-value dichotomy" (the notion that you can't derive values from facts) and the "naturalistic fallacy" (the notion that you can't define "good" in terms of natural properties). There are trivial differences among the variations, but they're essentially the same problem. Below I explain a major cause of the widespread confusion.
5. Dennis Prager, "Why Young Americans Can't Think Morally," September 20, 2011, http://www.dennisprager.com/columns.aspx?g=b5f5f8f2-7c6f-4c41-a48c-cfb8b97d48bb.

6. Ayn Rand, "The Objectivist Ethics," in *The Virtue of Selfishness* (New York: Signet, 1964), pp. 13–16.
7. Of course, people have free will and thus can pursue values that are contrary to the requirements of their life, but the fact remains that they don't *need* to pursue such values. If they don't want to live, they can simply stop acting and they will soon die. For more on this point, see Ayn Rand, "Causality Versus Duty" in *Philosophy: Who Needs It* (New York: Signet, 1982), pp. 95–101; and Craig Biddle, *Loving Life: The Morality of Self-Interest and the Facts that Support It* (Richmond: Glen Allen Press, 2002), pp. 43–52.
8. See Rand, "Collectivized Ethics," in *The Virtue of Selfishness*, p. 94.
9. The error of equating morality with altruism is not the original reason philosophers had trouble deriving morality from reality; the original reason is that philosophers observed correctly that we can't perceive "value" or "moral principle" or "ought," and they assumed that these things must therefore just be ideas detached from any fact in reality. (I address this aspect of the problem in a chapter titled "The Is–Ought Gap: Subjectivism's Technical Retreat" in *Loving Life*.) But the idea that we can't derive morality from reality *persists* in large part because people equate morality with altruism. Observe that few people doubt the existence of "precision" or "ambiguity" or "religion" or "economics" or the principles of physics or those of medicine or countless other things we can't see. The principles of morality remain elusive today largely because of the widespread practice of freezing the broad abstraction "morality" at the level of the narrow, concrete morality "altruism."
10. Thomas Nagel, *The Possibility of Altruism* (Princeton, NJ: Princeton University Press, 1978), p. 79.
11. Peter Singer, *A Darwinian Left* (New Haven, CT: Yale University Press, 1999), p. 56.
12. Rand, "The Ethics of Emergencies," in *The Virtue of Selfishness*, p. 50.

4. *Atlas Shrugged* and Ayn Rand's Morality of Egoism

1. Ayn Rand, *Journals of Ayn Rand*, edited by David Harriman (New York: Dutton, 1997), p. 610.
2. W. G. Maclagan, "Self and Others: A Defense of Altruism," *The Philosophical Quarterly*, vol. 4, no. 15 (April 1954): p. 122. Maclagan was an early 20th-century Scottish philosopher who taught at the University of Glasgow and was an ardent advocate of altruism.
3. Maclagan, "Self and Others," pp. 109–11.
4. Ayn Rand, *Philosophy: Who Needs It* (New York: Penguin, 1984), p. 61.
5. John Hospers, *Philosophical Analysis* (Upper Saddle River, NJ: Prentice-Hall, 1997), p. 259.

6. Ayn Rand, *The Virtue of Selfishness* (New York: Signet, 1962), p. 50.
7. Peter Singer, *A Darwinian Left* (New Haven, CT: Yale University Press, 1999), p. 56.
8. Thomas Nagel, *The Possibility of Altruism* (Princeton, NJ: Princeton University Press, 1978), p. 79.
9. Rand, *Philosophy: Who Needs It*, pp. 61–62.
10. Rand, *Virtue of Selfishness*, p. 27.
11. Ayn Rand, *For the New Intellectual* (New York: Signet, 1963), p. 129.
12. Rand, *Virtue of Selfishness*, pp. 82–83.
13. Rand, *Virtue of Selfishness*, pp. 126.
14. Rand, *Virtue of Selfishness*, pp. 108–10.
15. Rand, *Virtue of Selfishness*, pp. 110–13.
16. Ayn Rand, *The Voice of Reason* (New York: Meridian, 1989), p. 4.
17. Ayn Rand, *Capitalism: The Unknown Ideal* (New York: Signet, 1967), p. 19.
18. Rand, *Capitalism: The Unknown Ideal*, p. 19.
19. Rand, *Capitalism: The Unknown Ideal*, p. 136
20. Rand, *For the New Intellectual*, p. 142.
21. Rand, *Philosophy: Who Needs It*, p. 99.

5. Scientific Morality and the Streetlight Effect

1. This is my version of the fable known as the "streetlight effect." See "Streetlight Effect" at Wikipedia for its origins and other versions, https://en.wikipedia.org/wiki/Streetlight_effect.
2. See Alan Germani, "The Mystical Ethics of the New Atheists," *The Objective Standard* 3, no. 3 (Fall 2008): 25.
3. Sam Harris, *The End of Faith: Religion, Terror, and the Future of Reason* (New York: W. W. Norton & Company, 2004), 78.
4. Sam Harris, *The Moral Landscape: How Science Can Determine Human Values* (New York: Free Press, 2010), 82.
5. Daniel C. Dennett, *Breaking the Spell: Religion as a Natural Phenomenon* (New York: Penguin Books, 2006), 55.
6. Christopher Hitchens, "Going Godless: Atheists Rise," Good Morning America, November 14, 2007.
7. See also Craig Biddle, "Altruism: The Morality of Logical Fallacies," TOS Blog, May 22, 2006.
8. See Craig Biddle, "The Is-Altruism Dichotomy," *The Objective Standard* 8, no. 2 (Summer 2013): 46.
9. See Ayn Rand, *The Virtue of Selfishness* (New York: Signet, 1962); Craig Biddle, *Loving Life: The Morality of Self-Interest and the Facts That Support It* (Richmond: Glen Allen Press, 2002); or Craig Biddle, "Atlas Shrugged and Ayn Rand's Morality of Egoism," *The Objective Standard*7, no. 2 (Summer 2012): 31.

10. For a brief indication of how scientific morality is derived from observation and logic, see Craig Biddle, "Secular, Objective Morality: Look and See," *The Objective Standard* 12, no. 2 (Summer 2017): 47. For lengthier discussions, including more detail about the guidance provided by such morality, see Rand, *The Virtue of Selfishness*; and Biddle, *Loving Life*.

6. Purpose Comes from Reason, Not Religion

1. William Lane Craig, "The Absurdity of Life without God," https://www.reasonablefaith.org/writings/popular-writings/existence-nature-of-god/the-absurdity-of-life-without-god/.
2. Rick Warren, *The Purpose Driven Life: What on Earth Am I Here For?* (Grand Rapids, MI: Zondervan, 2002), 30.
3. Dennis Prager, "Secularism and the Meaningless Life," Orthodoxy Today, May 31, 2005, http://www.orthodoxytoday.org/articles5/PragerMeaningSecularism.php; "If There Is No God," Dennis Prager Show, August 19, 2008, https://www.dennisprager.com/if-there-is-no-god/.
4. Ben Shapiro, *The Right Side of History: How Reason and Moral Purpose Made the West Great* (New York: Broadside Books, 2019), 34–35.
5. Warren, *The Purpose Driven Life*, 18. It's worth noting the non sequitur here. Even if God did exist, and even if he made you, it wouldn't follow that you must live the life he wants for you. Your parents made you, and you have no moral obligation to live the life they want for you. You are a sovereign being with a mind and free will, and you can think and choose for yourself. And, according to rational morality, if you choose to live, you have a moral responsibility to think and choose for yourself.
6. Warren, *The Purpose Driven Life*, 17.
7. Warren, *The Purpose Driven Life*, 286.
8. See Scott Holleran, "Andrew Carnegie: The Richest Man in the World," *The Objective Standard* 5, no. 4 (Winter 2010): 47.
9. See Ross England, "Louis Pasteur: A Light That Brightens More and More," *The Objective Standard* 8, no. 4 (Winter 2013): 49.
10. See Katharine Hepburn, Wikipedia, https://en.wikipedia.org/wiki/Katharine_Hepburn.
11. See Ayn Rand, *Atlas Shrugged* (New York: Signet, 1957); and "The Objectivist Ethics," in *The Virtue of Selfishness* (New York: Signet, 1962).
12. For a brief indication of how the principle is derived, see my article "Secular, Objective Morality: Look and See," *The Objective Standard* 12, no. 2 (Summer 2017): 47. For a lengthier discussion, including a fleshed-out explanation of the so-called is–ought problem, see my book *Loving Life: The Morality of Self-Interest and the Facts That Support It* (Richmond: Glen Allen Press, 2002), especially chapter 2, "The Is–Ought Gap: Subjectivism's Technical Retreat," and chapter 3, "To Be or Not To Be: The Basic Choice."

13. Genesis 6:7.
14. Leviticus 24:16.
15. Deuteronomy 13:6–9.
16. Leviticus 20:13.
17. Leviticus 20:9, Deuteronomy 21:18–21.
18. Leviticus 25:44, Deuteronomy 15:12.
19. Deuteronomy 22:28–29, Numbers 31:15–18. Lest anyone claim that such commandments are found only in the Old Testament, bear in mind that the Old Testament is as much a part of Christianity as is the New Testament. According to Christianity, there is *one* God, and *all* of his laws, including those spelled out in the Old Testament, must be upheld. The New Testament is crystal clear about this. In the words of Jesus: "It is easier for heaven and earth to pass away than for one dot of the [Old Testament] Law to become void" (Luke 16:17). And: "Do not think that I have come to abolish the Law or the Prophets; I have not come to abolish them but to fulfill them. For truly, I say to you, until heaven and earth pass away, not an iota, not a dot, will pass from the Law until all is accomplished. Therefore whoever relaxes one of the least of these commandments and teaches others to do the same will be called least in the kingdom of heaven, but whoever does them and teaches them will be called great in the kingdom of heaven" (Matthew 5:17–19).
20. Al-Baqarah 2:191, At-Tawbah 9:5.
21. An-Nisa 4:24, Al-Ahzab 33:50.
22. E.g., see Rabbi Jonathan Sacks, "What is the Purpose of Life?," TorahCafe, https://www.torahcafe.com/rabbi-lord-jonathan-sacks/7-what-is-the-purpose-of-life-video_ad898c862.html; and William Lane Craig, "What Is The Purpose and Meaning of Life Without God?," https://www.youtube.com/watch?v=fKWKdiwDEcM. Regarding the latter, William Lane Craig's claim that if the universe has no purpose, then you can't have an ultimate purpose is ridiculous. It's like standing on a rock and saying, "If this rock has no purpose, then I can't have an ultimate purpose." Likewise, his claim to the effect that if life is not eternal—if it ends—then it is meaningless, makes no sense. That's like saying, "If this article ends, then it's meaningless."
23. Excerpted from Ayn Rand's radio interview with Raymond Newman on *The Raymond Newman Journal*, 1980.

7. Purpose, Value Hierarchies, and Happiness

1. Cf. Ayn Rand, interview by Alvin Toffler, *Playboy*, March 1964.
2. Ayn Rand, *Atlas Shrugged* (New York: Signet, 1992), pp. 92–93.
3. Ayn Rand, *Introduction to Objectivist Epistemology*, 2nd ed., edited by Harry Binswanger and Leonard Peikoff (New York: Penguin, 1990), p. 32.
4. Cf. Leonard Peikoff, *Objectivism: The Philosophy of Ayn Rand* (New York: Dutton, 1991), p. 298.

5. Rand, *Introduction to Objectivist Epistemology*, pp. 33–34.
6. See Ayn Rand, "The Objectivist Ethics," in *The Virtue of Selfishness* (New York: Signet, 1964), p. 29.

8. Egoism, Benevolence, and Generosity

1. For example, see on Greenpeace's website, "Keep It in the Ground," http://www.greenpeace.org/usa/global-warming/keep-it-in-the-ground/; and "Oil and Gas: Keep It in the Ground," http://www.greenpeace.org/international/en/campaigns/climate-change/End-oil-and-gas/.
2. Although some dictionaries define generosity as "the act or giving liberally" (or some equivalent), that doesn't capture the essence of the concept; the meaning of "liberally" is too vague. For more on the meaning and definition of the term, see Tara Smith, *Ayn Rand's Normative Ethics: The Virtuous Egoist* (Cambridge: Cambridge University Press, 2007), 257; and Ayn Rand, *Letters of Ayn Rand*, edited by Michael S. Berliner (New York: Dutton, 1995), 548.
3. To address a widespread confusion: Being honest is not necessarily the same thing as telling the truth. Honesty is the refusal to pretend that facts are other than they are, and it requires taking into account the full context of one's knowledge. In the light of that requirement, lying can be an act of honesty. For instance, if a burglar asks whether you have a hidden safe, and you lie to him by saying "no," you are not being dishonest; you're being honest; you are accounting for all of the relevant facts—including the fact that he has no right to your property. The burglar is being dishonest; he is ignoring relevant facts and pretending that he has a right to your property. Given the purpose of morality, which is to sustain and further human life, honesty does permit a person to lie—if the lie is necessary to protect a legitimate value from a person (or group) that seeks to steal, harm, or destroy it. For more on this, see my book *Loving Life: The Morality of Self-Interest and the Facts that Support It* (Richmond: Glen Allen Press, 2002), 83–85.
4. I speak here and throughout this article of one's *intended* hierarchy of values, which is not necessarily the same as one's *enacted* hierarchy. For a discussion of the difference between these, see "Purpose, Value Hierarchies, and Happiness," TOS Summer 2014, https://www.theobjectivestandard.com/issues/2014-summer/purpose-value-hierarchies-happiness/.
5. Holly Finn, "Think with Google: Missions that Matter," July 2011, https://www.thinkwithgoogle.com/marketing-resources/missions-that-matter/; Laszlo Bock, "Here's Google's Secret to Hiring the Best People," *Wired Business*, April 7, 2015, https://www.wired.com/2015/04/hire-like-google/; Michael B. Farrell, "The Google Mind: The Internet Powerhouse's Secrets for Hiring the Best," *The Boston Globe*, November 6, 2011, http://archive.boston.com/jobs/news/articles/2011/11/06/got_googliness_an_internet_powerhouse_shares_its_secrets_for_hiring_the_best/. For similar data regarding Amazon's hiring

practices and culture requirements, see Vernon Gunnarson, "3 Questions Amazon's CEO Asks Before Hiring Anyone," *The Daily Muse*, https://www.themuse.com/advice/3-questions-amazons-ceo-asks-before-hiring-anyone; Amazon's "Leadership Principles," https://www.amazon.jobs/principles; and Heather Wood Rudulph, "How to Get Hired at Amazon" *Cosmopolitan*, February 26, 2015, http://www.cosmopolitan.com/career/interviews/a36970/interview-insider-amazon-career-jobs/. For similar data regarding Apple, see Jonah Lehrer, "The Steve Jobs Approach to Teamwork," *Wired*, October 10, 2011, https://www.wired.com/2011/10/the-steve-jobs-approach-to-teamwork/; "7 Teamwork Lessons from Apple," TwentyOne Leadership, http://www.twentyoneleadership.com/resources/7-teamwork-lessons-from-apple/; and Maya Kosoff, "Apple Employees Reveal the 19 Best Things about Working for the World's Most Valuable Company," *Business Insider*, January 22, 2016, http://www.businessinsider.com/best-things-about-working-at-apple-2016-1/#the-salaries-are-pretty-good-for-many-positions-1.

6. Ultimately, this is an application of the onus of proof principle: The onus (or burden) of proof is on him who asserts (or assumes) the positive. Treating someone poorly assumes a positive—namely, that he has done something morally wrong and thus deserves to be treated poorly. In order *legitimately* to treat a person as having done something wrong, we must have *evidence* to that effect. To treat someone as guilty without evidence is to treat him as guilty for no reason, which is absurd and unjust. Thus, if we have no evidence that someone has done something wrong, we have a logical and moral responsibility to treat him as innocent. This applies to strangers as well as to people we know.
7. Dave Barry, *Dave Barry Turns 50* (New York: Ballantine, 1998), 185.
8. Ayn Rand, *Objectively Speaking: Ayn Rand Interviewed*, edited by Marlene Podritske and Peter Schwartz (Lanham, MD: Lexington Books, 2009), 160.
9. Ayn Rand, *Journals of Ayn Rand*, edited by David Harriman (New York: Penguin, 1997), 246.
10. Ayn Rand, "The Ethics of Emergencies," in *The Virtue of Selfishness* (New York: Signet, 1964), 54.
11. Cf. Smith, *Ayn Rand's Normative Ethics*, 256.
12. For a discussion of how to establish and maintain such a hierarchy, see "Purpose, Value Hierarchies, and Happiness."
13. The question of whether and when it can be selfish to risk one's life to help others, including strangers, is a subject for another essay. I expect to write something about this in the near future.
14. From the Q&A following Rand's Ford Hall Forum lecture, "Censorship: Local and Express," 1973, https://campus.aynrand.org/works/1973/01/01/censorship-local-and-express/page1.

9. Ayn Rand's Theory of Rights

1. Sarah Palin's speech at the Win America Back Conference, Independence, MO, May 1, 2010, http://www.youtube.com/watch?v=zLcQnvpamZU.
2. Rush Limbaugh, "The Smallest Minority on Earth," March 31, 2009, http://www.rushlimbaugh.com/home/daily/site_033109/content/01125110.guest.html.
3. Newt Gingrich, "A Conservative Plan for Victory," *Front Page Magazine*, April 6, 2005, http://www.frontpagemag.com/Articles/ReadArticle.asp?ID=17624.
4. "A Moment of Silence For Glenn Beck and James Dobson," January 26, 2009, http://malcantro.newsvine.com/_news/2009/01/26/2354412-a-moment-of-silence-for-glenn-beck-and-james-dobson.
5. E. J. Dionne Jr., "The Price of Liberty," *Washington Post*, April 15, 2003, http://www.washingtonpost.com/ac2/wp-dyn?pagename=article&contentId=A26667-2003Apr14¬Found=true.
6. Stephen Holmes and Cass R. Sunstein, *The Cost of Rights: Why Liberty Depends on Taxes* (New York: W. W. Norton & Company, 2000), 17.
7. Quoted in Sidney Hook, *The Paradoxes of Freedom* (Berkeley: University of California Press, 1962), 8.
8. The phrases "civil rights," "procedural rights," "legal rights," and the like properly include qualifiers in recognition of the fact that the concept of "rights" *proper* is a moral concept.
9. John Locke, *Second Treatise of Civil Government* (1690), chap. 2, sec. 6, http://www.constitution.org/jl/2ndtr02.htm.
10. Thomas Jefferson to William Johnson, June 12, 1823, in *Writings of Thomas Jefferson*, edited by Andrew A. Lipscomb and Albert Ellery (Washington, DC: Thomas Jefferson Memorial Association, 1905), http://press-pubs.uchicago.edu/founders/documents/v1ch15s67.html.
11. Thomas Jefferson, *Opinion on French Treaties*, 1793, TeachingAmericanHistory.org, http://teachingamericanhistory.org/library/index.asp?document=623.
12. First Draft of the Declaration of Independence, *Papers of Thomas Jefferson*, Princeton University, http://www.princeton.edu/~tjpapers/declaration/declaration.html; letter to Major John Cartwright, June 5, 1824, *Letters of Thomas Jefferson*, University of Virginia Library, http://etext.virginia.edu/etcbin/toccer-new2?id=JefLett.sgm&images=images/modeng&data=/texts/english/modeng/parsed&tag=public&part=276&division=div1.
13. Thomas Jefferson, *A Summary View of the Rights of British America*, 1774, in *Writings of Thomas Jefferson*, http://press-pubs.uchicago.edu/founders/documents/v1ch14s10.html.
14. Locke, *Second Treatise*, chap. 2, sec. 6.
15. This meaning is corroborated throughout Locke's writing, including in his definition of natural law as "the command of the divine will, knowable by the light of nature, indicating what is and is not consonant with a rational nature,

and by that very fact commanding or prohibiting." (*Questions Concerning the Law of Nature* [Ithaca, NY: Cornell University Press, 2nd ed., 2008], 101.)

16. Jefferson, *Opinion on French Treaties.*
17. Thomas Jefferson, legal argument in the case of Howell vs. Netherland 2, 1770, in the *Works of Thomas Jefferson*, vol. 1, federal ed. (New York and London, G.P. Putnam's Sons, 1904–5), http://oll.libertyfund.org/?option=com_staticxt&staticfile=show.php%3Ftitle=800&chapter=85803&layout=html&Itemid=27.
18. *The Works of Alexander Hamilton: Miscellanies, 1774–1789, Vol. 2*,edited by John C. Hamilton (New York: John F. Trow, 1854), 43.
19. Quoted in Scott Douglas Gerber, *To Secure These Rights: The Declaration of Independence and Constitutional Interpretation* (New York: NYU Press, 1996), 106.
20. John Adams, *Papers of John Adams*, vol. 1 (Cambridge: Harvard University Press, 1977), 112.
21. Ayn Rand, "Conservatism: An Obituary," in *Capitalism: The Unknown Ideal* (New York: Signet, 1967), 197.
22. Alasdair MacIntyre, *After Virtue*, 2nd ed. (Notre Dame: University of Notre Dame Press, 1984), 68–70.
23. For elaboration, see Ayn Rand, *The Virtue of Selfishness* (New York: Signet, 1964); Craig Biddle, *Loving Life: The Morality of Self-Interest and the Facts that Support It* (Richmond: Glen Allen Press, 2002); Tara Smith, *Viable Values: A Study of Life as the Root and Reward of Morality* (Lanham, MD: Rowman & Littlefield, 2000); Tara Smith, *Ayn Rand's Normative Ethics: The Virtuous Egoist* (Cambridge: Cambridge University Press, 2007).
24. Ayn Rand, "The Objectivist Ethics," in *The Virtue of Selfishness*, 13.
25. Rand, "The Objectivist Ethics," 16.
26. Rand, "The Objectivist Ethics," 16.
27. Rand, "The Objectivist Ethics," 16.
28. For a fuller discussion of this derivation, see Rand, *The Virtue of Selfishness*; Biddle, *Loving Life*; and Smith, *Viable Values*.
29. This question, incidentally, slashes away the entire duty-based approach to ethics that Immanuel Kant and company advocate. If man needs values, then he must need them for some life-serving purpose. What else could "need" mean? If man doesn't need values, then there is no point in telling him which code of values he should adopt.
30. Rand, "The Objectivist Ethics," 18.
31. Cf. Ayn Rand, "Philosophical Detection," in *Philosophy: Who Needs It* (New York: Signet, 1984), 22, footnote.
32. See Ayn Rand, "Introducing Objectivism," in *The Voice of Reason* (New York: Meridian, 1990), 4.
33. See Leonard Peikoff, *Objectivism: The Philosophy of Ayn Rand* (New York: Dutton, 1991), 229–30.

34. Rand, "The Objectivist Ethics," 32–33.
35. Rand, "The Objectivist Ethics," 22–23.
36. Of course, a person can act irrationally on occasion and still remain alive. But such actions are nevertheless contrary to the requirements of his life; they do not advance it; they retard, stifle, or thwart it to some extent. For instance, one can shoot heroin into one's veins occasionally and not die immediately, but, unless there is some genuine medicinal value in doing so, the drug will have a negative effect on one's life. Likewise, one can fail to exert the effort necessary to achieve the career or the lifestyle one wants, but then one will not thrive to the extent that one could have if one had exerted the effort.
37. Cf. Ayn Rand, *For the New Intellectual* (New York: Signet, 1963), 134.
38. Ayn Rand, "America's Persecuted Minority: Big Business," in *Capitalism: The Unknown Ideal* (New York: Signet, 1967), 46.
39. Rob Hotakainen, "In the Face of Death: Terminally Ill Patients Want Quicker Access to Experimental Drugs," *Boulder Weekly*, May 29, 2008, http://boulder-weekly.com/archives/20080529/onlineexclusivebandofsisters.html.
40. Ayn Rand, "Man's Rights," in *The Virtue of Selfishness*, 108.
41. Rand, "Man's Rights," 110.
42. Rand, "Man's Rights," 110.
43. Rand, "Man's Rights," 113.
44. Ayn Rand, "The Wreckage of the Consensus," in *Capitalism: The Unknown Ideal*, 227.
45. Some natural rights theorists have claimed that natural moral law—and thus natural rights—are inherent in reality apart from or regardless of God's existence. For instance, Hugo Grotius, the 17th-century Dutch Jurist, who influenced Locke, wrote that natural moral law "would have a degree of validity even if we should concede that which cannot be conceded without the utmost wickedness, that there is no God, or that the affairs of men are of no concern to him." But, to my knowledge, neither Grotius nor anyone else (with the exception of Ayn Rand) has ever shown what these natural moral laws are, proven their specific content, or demonstrated how they give rise to rights.
46. And it's a good thing that rights are *not* inherent. If rights were somehow inherent in man by virtue of his being man, then we could never punish people who violate rights—because using retaliatory force against them would violate the "rights" that they "inherently" have and that they thus always retain by virtue of being human. Because Rand's theory is based on and derived from the observable requirements of man's life, it is not afflicted with contradictions regarding those requirements. On Rand's theory, rights are inalienable, in that others cannot take away or nullify one's rights; but they are also *forfeitable*, in that one can relinquish one's own rights by violating the rights of others. If and to the extent that a person violates the rights of others, he relinquishes his own rights and may be punished accordingly. His choice to violate rights places him outside the purpose of the principle and thus the scope of its protection. Again, one cannot claim the protection of a principle that one repudiates in action.

10. Individualism vs. Collectivism

1. A. Maurice Low, "What is Socialism? III: An Explanation of 'The Rights' Men Enjoy in a State of Civilized Society," *The North American Review*, vol. 197, no. 688 (March 1913), 406.
2. Letter to Thomas Auld, September 3, 1848, in *Frederick Douglass: Selected Speeches and Writings* (Chicago: Lawrence Hill Books, 1999). Also available online at http://www.yale.edu/glc/archive/1121.htm.
3. John Dewey, "The Ethics of Democracy," in *The Early Works of John Dewey, Volume 1, 1882–1898: Early Essays and Leibniz's New Essays, 1882–1888*, edited by Jo Ann Boydston and George E. Axetell (Carbondale, IL: Southern Illinois University Press, 2008), 232.
4. The roots of this idea can be found in Plato's *The Republic*.
5. Cf. Ayn Rand, *Introduction to Objectivist Epistemology*, 2nd ed., edited by Harry Binswanger and Leonard Peikoff (New York: Penguin, 1990), 35.
6. Helen E. Longino, "Knowledge in Social Theories of Science," in *Socializing Epistemology: The Social Dimensions of Knowledge*, edited by Frederick F. Schmitt (Lanham, MD: Rowman & Littlefield, 1994), 139, 142–43.
7. Low, "What is Socialism? III," 405–6.
8. Ayn Rand, "Textbook of Americanism," in *The Ayn Rand Column* (New Milford, CT: Second Renaissance Books, 1998), 90.
9. David Callahan, "The Biggest Idea in Obama's Speech: A Common Good," The Demos Weblog, January 26, 2012, http://www.policyshop.net/home/2012/1/26/the-biggest-idea-in-obamas-speech-a-common-good.html.
10. Michael Tomasky, "Party in Search of a Notion," *The American Prospect*, April 18, 2006. Available online at http://prospect.org/article/party-search-notion.
11. Barack Obama, Keynote Address, Sojourners/Call to Renewal-sponsored Pentecost conference, June 2006, http://www.sojo.net/index.cfm?action=news.display_article&mode=C&NewsID=5454; Penny Starr, "Obama Calls Health Care a 'Moral Obligation,' But Pro-lifers Say Tax Money for Abortions Is 'Moral' Issue," August 21, 2009, http://www.cnsnews.com/news/article/52844; Obama, Commencement Speech at Wesleyan University, 2008, http://www.wesleyan.edu/newsrel/announcements/rc_2008/obama_speech.html.
12. Hank De Zutter, "What Makes Obama Run?," *Chicago Reader*, December 7, 1995. Available online at http://www.chicagoreader.com/chicago/what-makes-obama-run/Content?oid=889221.
13. Rick Santorum, *It Takes a Family* (Intercollegiate Studies Institute, 2005), 14–15.
14. Jonathan Rauch, "A Frothy Mixture of Collectivism and Conservatism: America's Anti-Reagan Isn't Hillary Clinton. It's Rick Santorum," *Reason Magazine*, September 6, 2005. Available online at http://reason.com/archives/2005/09/06/a-frothy-mixture-of-collectivi.
15. Ayn Rand, "The Cashing-In: The Student 'Rebellion,'" in *Capitalism: The Unknown Ideal* (New York: Signet, 1967), 269.

11. Capitalism and the Moral High Ground

1. "Redistribution of Wealth," YouTube video, accessed November 30, 2008, http://www.youtube.com/watch?v=QJySlWJNisM.
2. "Maxine Waters threatens to nationalize U.S. oil industries," YouTube video, accessed November 30, 2008, http://www.youtube.com/watch?v=PUaY3LhJ-IQ.
3. Quoted in Pete Du Pont, "Socialism's Last Redoubt," *Wall Street Journal*, February 16, 2005, http://www.opinionjournal.com/columnists/pdupont/?id=110006296.
4. Karl Marx, "On the Jewish Question," in *Karl Marx: Selected Writings*, 2nd ed., edited by David McLellan (New York: Oxford University Press, 2000), 60.
5. "Selfishness: Obama Wages New Attack On Those Who Don't Want Higher Taxes," YouTube video, accessed November 30, 2008, http://www.youtube.com/watch?v=v8Th4UvADxc.
6. George Gilder, "Moral Sources of Capitalism," in *The Essential Neoconservative Reader*, edited by Mark Gerson (Reading, MA: Addison-Wesley, 1996), 155, 152, 159.
7. Michael Novak, "*From* the Spirit of Democratic Capitalism," in *Essential Neoconservative Reader*, 127.
8. Cf. Ayn Rand, *Capitalism: The Unknown Ideal* (New York: Signet, 1967), 19. For elaboration on how fraud and other forms of indirect force constitute *physical* force, see Craig Biddle, *Loving Life: The Morality of Self-Interest and the Facts that Support It* (Richmond: Glen Allen Press, 2002), 104–112.
9. Cf. Ayn Rand, "Textbook of Americanism," in *The Ayn Rand Column*, 2nd ed. (New Milford, CT: Second Renaissance Books, 1998), 86.
10. The closest system to capitalism was that of late 19th-century America, which, consequently, was an era of unparalleled innovation and economic growth.
11. Cf. Ayn Rand, *For the New Intellectual* (New York: Signet, 1963), 120; and *The Virtue of Selfishness* (New York: Signet, 1962), 22–23.
12. Cf. *For the New Intellectual*, 182; and *Capitalism: The Unknown Ideal*, 17.
13. Cf. *The Virtue of Selfishness*, 50.
14. Peter Singer, *A Darwinian Left* (New Haven: Yale University Press, 1999), 56.
15. Thomas Nagel, *The Possibility of Altruism* (Princeton: Princeton University Press, 1978), 79.
16. Ayn Rand, *Philosophy: Who Needs It* (New York: Signet, 1982), 61.
17. Rand, *Philosophy: Who Needs It*, 61–62.
18. As to the very few people who are genuinely incapacitated and thus unable to support themselves by any means—such as those who are severely mentally retarded—what they need is not the alleged benefits of people's sacrifices, but the actual benefits of people's freedom to think and produce such that they can afford to offer charity, if they so choose.
19. See *The Virtue of Selfishness*, 162.

20. For the scientific derivation of this principle, see *The Virtue of Selfishness*, 13–18; and *Loving Life: The Morality of Self-Interest and the Facts that Support It*, 43–52.
21. See *The Virtue of Selfishness* and *Loving Life*.

12. The Argument from Intimidation

1. Ayn Rand, "From My 'Future File,'" in *The Ayn Rand Letter* 3, no. 66 (September 23, 1974).
2. Ayn Rand, "The Argument from Intimidation," in *The Virtue of Selfishness*, 162–63.
3. Paul Krugman, "Galt, Gold and God," *New York Times*, August 23, 2012, https://www.nytimes.com/2012/08/24/opinion/krugman-galt-gold-and-god.html.
4. Kevin D. Williamson, "The Parochial Progressive Obsession with Ayn Rand," *National Review*, December 14, 2016, https://www.nationalreview.com/2016/12/progressive-ayn-rand-obsession-misguided/.
5. Heidi N. Moore, "Capitalism Shrugged: Should Ayn Rand Be Required Reading?," *Wall Street Journal*, April 11, 2008, https://blogs.wsj.com/deals/2008/04/11/capitalism-shrugged-should-ayn-rand-be-required-reading/.
6. John Gray, "Atheism Wars," *Playboy*, April 2013, 49–53.
7. Rand did not reject compassion. She rejected compassion toward the morally guilty. As she put it, "I regard compassion as proper *only* toward those who are innocent victims, but not toward those who are morally guilty. If one feels compassion for the victims of a concentration camp, one cannot feel it for the torturers. If one does feel compassion for the torturers, it is an act of moral treason toward the victims." ["Playboy Interview: Ayn Rand," interviewed by Alvin Toffler, *Playboy*, March 1964, 35–43.]
8. Sam Harris, How to Lose Readers (Without Even Trying), SamHarris.org, August 24, 2011, https://samharris.org/how-to-lose-readers-without-even-trying/.
9. Rand, "The Argument from Intimidation," 164.

Index

About the Author

Craig Biddle is a writer and speaker focusing on the morality of self-interest, the philosophy of Objectivism, and the nature of principled thinking. He is editor of *The Objective Standard*, the preeminent source for commentary from an Objectivist perspective; author of *Loving Life: The Morality of Self-Interest and the Facts that Support It*; and author of more than two hundred articles on philosophy, culture, and politics. His books in progress are "Rational Self-Interest for Teens: Moral Truths Your Parents, Preachers, and Teachers Don't Want You to Know" and "Thinking in Principles: Using Your Mind in Service of Your Life, Liberty, and Happiness."

Biddle speaks regularly at conferences, on college campuses, and to community groups. He also serves on the board of directors of the Prometheus Foundation, a nonprofit dedicated to helping people discover and understand Objectivism, so they can use it to live rich, meaningful, and happy lives.

His website is CraigBiddle.com.

Made in the USA
San Bernardino, CA
06 September 2019